T0323923

Cambridge Elements ☰

Elements in the Philosophy of Mathematics
edited by
Penelope Rush
University of Tasmania
Stewart Shapiro
The Ohio State University

INTRODUCING THE PHILOSOPHY OF MATHEMATICAL PRACTICE

Jessica Carter
Aarhus University

CAMBRIDGE
UNIVERSITY PRESS

Shaftesbury Road, Cambridge CB2 8EA, United Kingdom

One Liberty Plaza, 20th Floor, New York, NY 10006, USA

477 Williamstown Road, Port Melbourne, VIC 3207, Australia

314–321, 3rd Floor, Plot 3, Splendor Forum, Jasola District Centre, New Delhi – 110025, India

103 Penang Road, #05–06/07, Visioncrest Commercial, Singapore 238467

Cambridge University Press is part of Cambridge University Press & Assessment, a department of the University of Cambridge.

We share the University's mission to contribute to society through the pursuit of education, learning and research at the highest international levels of excellence.

www.cambridge.org
Information on this title: www.cambridge.org/9781009479387

DOI: 10.1017/9781009076067

First published 2024

A catalogue record for this publication is available from the British Library.

ISBN 978-1-009-47938-7 Hardback
ISBN 978-1-009-07478-0 Paperback
ISSN 2399-2883 (online)
ISSN 2514-3808 (print)

Introducing the Philosophy of Mathematical Practice

Elements in the Philosophy of Mathematics

DOI: 10.1017/9781009076067
First published online: December 2024

Jessica Carter
Aarhus University

Author for correspondence: Jessica Carter, jessica@css.au.dk

Abstract: This Element introduces a young field, the 'philosophy of mathematical practice'. It offers a general characterisation of the approach to the philosophy of mathematics that takes mathematical practice seriously and contrasts it with 'mathematical philosophy'. The latter is traced back to Bertrand Russell and the orientation referred to as 'scientific philosophy' that was active between 1850 and 1930. To give a better sense of the field, the Element further includes two examples of topics studied: mathematical structuralism and visual thinking in mathematics. These are in part presented from a methodological point of view, focussing on mathematics as an activity and questions related to how mathematics develops. In addition, the Element contains several examples from mathematics, both historical and contemporary, to illustrate and support the philosophical points.

Keywords: philosophy of mathematical practice, mathematical philosophy, mathematical structuralism, visual thinking in mathematics, diagrams

ISBNs: 9781009479387 (HB), 9781009074780 (PB), 9781009076067 (OC)
ISSNs: 2399-2883 (online), 2514-3808 (print)

Contents

Introduction   1

1 Different Approaches to Philosophy of Mathematics   3

2 Structure in Mathematics   20

3 Visual Thinking in Mathematics   43

   Conclusion   61

   References   64

Introduction

Mathematics is a fascinating yet mysterious field. Some are drawn to it because of its rigour and because it yields absolute truths. Others are taken by mathematics' capacity to describe our complex world in simple relations. When engaging with mathematics, however, questions arise. One might wonder how we were even able to develop and grasp all of the complex structures that constitute contemporary mathematics. A related question concerns the nature of the relations between elementary mathematical activities such as counting and measuring and the modern abstract theories of mathematics – if there are any such relations. Mathematics has a language of its own with technical terms, notations that are used to write expressions in a compact and convenient form, and a variety of visual representations such as figures and diagrams. This special language is also part of what makes mathematics difficult to understand. In this light, one may ask: What is the role of the notation and visual representations – are they essential components of contemporary mathematics or merely useful devices? Could it also be that they somehow aid our discovery of mathematical facts? These are examples of questions that are of interest to the philosopher of mathematical practice and some of them will be addressed in this Element.

The main purpose of this Element is to introduce the field of philosophy that takes as its starting point the practice of mathematics. This is a difficult task – in part since the field is still young. This means that, even though there is some consensus as to what the philosophy of mathematical practice (abbreviated as PMP) may designate, scholars claiming to be in the field still characterise it in quite distinct ways. One way to describe PMP is to contrast it with mainstream philosophy of mathematics. The following four general trends give a rough idea. First, PMP aims to extend the topics that can be studied as part of the philosophy of mathematics beyond the traditional questions concerning the foundations and ontology of mathematics. Second, philosophers of practice often take interest in more specific questions, such as 'What is a mathematical explanation?', in contrast to the broader pictures that one finds in philosophy. Third, methods drawn upon may be different. Philosophy of mathematical practice is historically sensitive, analyses case studies, and sometimes even refers to scientific or empirical results whereas mainstream philosophy of mathematics belongs to analytic philosophy and develops and is based on formal tools. Finally, mathematics is often portrayed as static, a collection of eternal truths, in mainstream philosophy. In PMP, we are (also) interested in mathematics' dynamic character, how concepts are defined, proofs are found, and so on, stressing that mathematics is an activity done by human agents. This *is* a rough sketch and does not capture the richness of the field. Philosophy of mathematical practice, for example, also draws on analytic tools and in certain cases seeks to formulate 'big pictures'.

The Element comprises three sections. Each section can be read independently, but there are examples that are referred to across the sections. The first section introduces the 'philosophy of mathematical practice' from a general point of view. The section provides an outline of some of the different approaches to PMP mainly through an analysis of what 'practice' refers to.

In addition to PMP, scholars have also used 'mathematical philosophy' to characterise the type of philosophy of mathematics that interacts with mathematical practice proper. This term was used by Bertrand Russell about a century ago and refers to the general movement, scientific philosophy, which was active between 1850 and 1930. There are interesting similarities (as well as differences) between this movement and the current PMP, some of which will be pointed out.

The ensuing two sections treat in more detail two examples of work in the philosophy of mathematical practice. The two topics are Mathematical Structuralism and Visual Thinking in Mathematics. One motivation to adopt a structuralist position stems from developments within mathematics itself. Structuralism therefore is an exemplary case of a philosophical position inspired by mathematical practice. Emphasising a dynamic conception of mathematics, I focus on methodological aspects of structuralism. This includes using the axiomatic method as a tool to create structures and to organise mathematics in various ways. Furthermore, I consider the role of relations in mathematics on a 'global' scale which entails understanding mathematical structuralism in a broader sense than is typical in the philosophy of mathematics.

Section 3 contains a brief historical introduction to the use of diagrams in mathematics, starting with the observation that diagrams formed an essential component of Greek mathematics. Euclid's *Elements* was long regarded as the paradigm for how mathematics should be studied and presented, and so geometry served for many centuries as a foundation for mathematics. However, during the eighteenth century, this picture gradually shifted, and at the turn of the twentieth century one finds explicit statements that proofs should not rely on geometric intuition nor be based on diagrams. In the latter part of the twentieth century, philosophers contested this view, noticing the prevalence of diagrams in mathematical practice. Consequently, scholars began investigating the role that figures, or diagrams, play. We will consider some contributions that examine the use of diagrams in proofs, noting that each is based on a careful analysis of exemplary cases and that diagram-based reasoning can be supported by formal arguments. Finally, I will highlight some of the advantages that diagrams offer over other types of representations.

1 Different Approaches to Philosophy of Mathematics

There are different ways in which mathematics presents itself and gives rise to philosophical reflections. One might think of mathematics (for example, at a certain point in time) as a collection of theories that establish relations between concepts, formulated in terms of propositions, and that we have knowledge of a proposition in case there is a proof of it. Questions that this picture might raise concern the nature of the involved mathematical concepts, how to account for the apparent necessity of mathematical propositions, and which requirements should be stated for arguments to be accepted as rigorous proofs. This is a static conception of mathematics. In contrast, one might be interested in mathematics as an activity wondering, for example, how concepts are developed and theories formed. One might also enquire about various epistemic concerns such as why mathematicians value multiple proofs of the same theorem. One might think that this division – between a static and dynamic conception of mathematics – is simple and that the questions they give rise to as well as the methods employed to respond to them are disjoint. This turns out not to be true, as we shall see.

The label 'The philosophy of mathematical practice' (PMP) will be reserved for topics within the philosophy of mathematics that explicitly address themes that are tied to the practice of mathematics, interests of mathematicians (present and past) that are related to their mathematical practice, or challenges posed by the content of mathematics (broadly construed). 'Practice' may, but need not, imply an underlying assumption that mathematics is done by human agents. There are a number of different approaches to the philosophy of mathematics that take an 'agent based' perspective, that is, perspectives based on the fact that mathematics is done by human beings or is the outcome of human activities. Such a point of view affects, among other things, how knowledge is characterised. I return to this point in Section 1.2. Other approaches to PMP insist that philosophical reflections are informed by mathematics itself, for example, mathematical theories, concepts, how proofs convince, are found or presented. Furthermore, 'philosophy that is informed by mathematics' could also mean that mathematics itself provides the tools to solve philosophical problems. It may not be entirely clear what I mean by these brief descriptions, but the current and two consecutive sections are intended to give some concrete examples that illustrate these points.

One could also ask how the 'philosophy of mathematical practice' differs from the philosophy of mathematics. This is, indeed, a relevant, but difficult, question. One thing that makes it complicated is the many different traditions (both past and present) of thinking about mathematics. In light of this, 'the philosophy of mathematics' cannot refer to a single approach. This entails that

4 The Philosophy of Mathematics

what I will be characterising as the 'philosophy of mathematical practice' may be compatible with both past and existing traditions. Aldo Antonelli (2001), characterising what he refers to as 'mathematical philosophy', makes a related point when noting that mathematical philosophy has been practised by a number of past thinkers from Plato to Hilbert. Antonelli contrasts mathematical philosophy to contributions that are exclusively concerned with ontological questions, 'the epistemology of mathematical propositions, or the necessary status of mathematical truths' (2001, p. 1) – questions that elsewhere are claimed to belong to mainstream philosophy of mathematics.

Early proponents of a 'practice oriented' approach objected to the one-sided focus on foundational questions and the use of formal tools, namely formal logic and set theory, when dealing with them. Some of them, referred to as 'mavericks', even claimed that mathematics does not need foundations; see Mancosu (2008a) for an elaboration. Less radical philosophers have instead urged that the range of topics and questions considered should be extended. A further requirement is that answers to these questions should draw on relevant mathematical theories (that go beyond arithmetic and set theory).

In this first section I introduce the philosophy of mathematical practice (PMP) and mathematical philosophy that is related to it. 'Mathematical philosophy' has recently been used to characterise philosophical work that employs mathematical tools to address problems in mathematics (Weber 2013) and, as mentioned earlier, to offer a particular perspective on the philosophy of mathematics (Antonelli 2001). The label was coined by Bertrand Russell (1919) and appears in the title of his book *Introduction to Mathematical Philosophy*.[1] Russell's 'mathematical philosophy' can be seen as part of the general movement 'scientific philosophy' which started in the mid nineteenth century. Through the influence of Russell and others, it transformed into what is today known as analytic philosophy.[2] Mathematical philosophy as characterised by Antonelli can be seen as a version of PMP. It may therefore seem odd that it can be traced back to Russell who has been highly influential in the development of analytic philosophy and is one of the fathers of the logicist programme, one of the foundational schools. Both the foundational schools and formal tools used in analytic philosophy, or at least certain versions of these, have been criticised by

---

[1] 'Mathematical philosophy' has a number of different interpretations. It could mean the use of mathematical, or formal tools in philosophy (cf. Munich Center for Mathematical Philosophy), that views on mathematics inform one's philosophy (as in the writings of C.S. Peirce), or as a view on the philosophy of mathematics that takes mathematical practice seriously.

[2] Some of the early philosophers usually mentioned as the originators of analytic philosophy are Moore, Russell, and Wittgenstein. Wittgenstein was in particular influenced by Russell and Frege.

the mavericks and other precursors to PMP. If one considers the original motivation and general ideas of scientific or mathematical philosophy, however, it turns out that they resonate with ideas of PMP. This need not imply that the particular outcomes, that is, the positions of these orientations have to overlap and that there is agreement on every point. Not everyone agrees with Russell, for example, that mathematics is the same as formal logic (Russell 1901).

Section 1.1 briefly introduces mathematical philosophy as it was conceived by Russell and the context of scientific philosophy. The main point is to illustrate that scientific philosophy and Russell's mathematical philosophy contain certain ideas that are shared with PMP. Another main point will be to illustrate that what the philosophy of mathematics is, which topics are of interest to philosophers, and what methods are used change over time. Section 1.2 discusses general themes of the philosophy of mathematical practice.

1.1 Scientific and Mathematical Philosophy

In the introduction to a special issue of *Topoi*, Antonelli defines 'mathematical philosophy' as *that area of philosophical reflection that is contiguous to, and interactive with, mathematical practice proper* (Antonelli 2001, p. 1). To be interactive with mathematical practice entails that one draws on relevant parts of mathematics: *Paraphrasing Kant, one could say that mathematics without philosophy is blind, and philosophy without mathematics is empty* (Antonelli 2001, p. 1).[3] Antonelli further claims that philosophy that is not informed by mathematical practice risks becoming either legislative or apologetic. In contrast, mathematical philosophy 'is respectful of, but not subsidiary to, current mathematical practice. It engages the issues, points out conceptual tensions, and highlights unexpected consequences. Mathematical philosophy positions itself neither above nor below mathematics, but rather on a par with it, taking the role of an equal interlocutor' (Antonelli 2001, p. 1). Antonelli attributes the term 'mathematical philosophy' to Russell, to whom we now turn.

Mathematical philosophy is part of scientific philosophy that arose around the mid nineteenth century as a reaction against the post-Kantian German idealism of, for example, Hegel and Schelling and, in the case of Russell, also nineteenth-century British idealism.[4] The scientific philosophers wished instead to base philosophy on the methods of science that had proven far more successful. The former grand systems of philosophy were regarded as individualistic and subjective in contrast to the scientific methods that were taken to be progressive, collaborative, and objective.

---

[3] See Kant's *Critique of Pure Reason*, A51/B51.
[4] Further details can be found in Richardson (1997) and Preston (n.d.).

The label 'scientific philosophy' was used by Hermann von Helmholtz in a famous talk celebrating Kant in 1855 in Königsberg on the occasion of the dedication of a monument to Kant. In this talk, Helmholtz noted the enmity and distrust between science and philosophy. He urged instead that they should collaborate. According to Helmholtz, philosophers should turn to the theory of knowledge and base their theories on the recent developments of relevant fields (i.e., psychology and physiology) instead of building grand systems of metaphysics. The list of scientific philosophers is long and among twentieth-century philosophers we find Schlick, Carnap, and Quine (Friedman 2012), Russell, Husserl, and the early Heidegger (Richardson 1997).

It is clear from this list that 'scientific philosophy' covers quite diverse approaches to philosophy. What makes them 'scientific' is summed up by Heidegger in a lecture given in 1925 (quoted from Richardson (1997), p. 441):

1. Because it is a philosophy of the sciences, that is, because it is a theory of scientific knowledge, because it has as its actual object the fact of science.
2. Because by way of this inquiry into the structure of already given sciences it secures its own theme that it investigates in accordance with its own method, while it itself no longer lapses into the domain of reflection characteristic of the particular sciences. It is "scientific" because it acquires its own domain and its own method. At the same time, the method maintains its security by its constant orientation to the factual conduct of the sciences themselves. Speculation aimed at world views is thereby avoided.[5]

While the scientific philosophers shared a common enemy in the former 'speculative world views', there was little agreement on which part of science or scientific method should replace them. According to Richardson, Russell has to a large extent influenced how scientific philosophy is understood today, that 'scientific' means using the relevant logical tools (p. 424). He notes, however, that quite different interpretations existed. Husserl, for example, also regarded himself as a scientific philosopher (and is later mentioned by Heidegger as belonging to that tradition). To Husserl, the scientific method used in his phenomenology consisted in analysing 'pure consciousness'. In relation to mathematics, one might also take the point of view that 'scientific' refers to mathematics itself in the sense that mathematical or meta-mathematical tools are drawn on when solving philosophical problems. Referring to Hilbert's

---

[5] I omit Heidegger's third point, which places the scientific philosophers in the tradition of phenomenology, or the science of consciousness.

contributions to meta-mathematics, Hourya Benis-Sinaceur (2018) argues that Hilbert can be considered as a scientific philosopher in this latter sense.[6]

An important part of the general scientific method, and an idea that is shared among the scientific philosophers, is that scientific questions are solved by collaborative efforts and that this allows researchers to split big problems into smaller and manageable ones (Richardson, p. 434). Here formulated by Russell:

> It is chiefly owing to this fact that philosophy, unlike science, has hitherto been unprogressive, because each original philosopher has had to begin the work again from the beginning, without being able to accept anything definite from the work of his predecessors. A scientific philosophy such as I wish to recommend will be piecemeal and tentative like other sciences ... What is feasible is the understanding of general forms, and the division of general problems into a number of separate and less baffling questions. "Divide and conquer" is the maxim of success here as elsewhere. (Russell 1914, p. 113)

In contrast to scientific investigations, however, the scientific philosopher must not rely on empirical facts:

> [a] philosophical proposition must be such as can be neither proved nor disproved by empirical evidence. Too often we find in philosophical books arguments based upon the course of history, or the convolutions of the brain, or the eyes of shell-fish. Special and accidental facts of this kind are irrelevant to philosophy, which must make only such assertions as would be equally true however the actual world were constituted. (Russell 1914, p. 111)

Philosophy should be based on general propositions (which is possible with the help from logic) that are a priori.

An important component of Russell's mathematical philosophy was his use of the recently developed tools from logic, most notably by Gottlob Frege. Frege introduced quantificational logic which, in addition to quantifiers, employs the concept of a function that can be applied to one or multiple arguments. Whereas propositions were earlier analysed in the form 'predicate and subject', Frege's logic allows one to use the components 'A(d)' or 'A(x)' where A stands for some property and 'd' an individual to which the property

---

[6] Benis-Sinaceur (2018) focuses on Hilbert's use of the Kantian notion of critique and explains in detail how Hilbert puts his axiomatic method and proof theory under the banner of critique (referring to, e.g., Hilbert's *Grundlagen der Geometrie* 1899, and 'Axiomatic Thought' 1918). Hilbert refers to the investigation of the foundation and logical structures of geometry in his *Foundations of Geometry* as 'an analysis of the intuition of space' (p. 27). In contrast to Kant's view, Hilbert's 'intuition' is objective (and associated with his 'finitist attitude'): '*intuition is rooted in perceiving sensory signs outside of the mind*'. Put briefly, Hilbert solves the problems of mathematics by drawing on meta-mathematical tools, replacing the role of philosophy with mathematics itself (Benis-Sinaceur 2018, p. 35).

is ascribed. In this way, it is possible to capture the logical structure of sentences of the form 'For all x P(x)' or 'There exists an x such that P(x)' for some predicate P (and, of course, much more complicated sentences using nested quantification and relational symbols). The new logic was introduced as part of Frege's logicist programme that intended to demonstrate that the theory of numbers could be reduced to logic. It is well-known that Frege's original attempt failed: Russell discovered that one of Frege's assumptions gave rise to the paradox known as Russell's paradox. The assumption allows one to consider the extension of any conceivable concept.[7] If one considers the property of 'not belonging to itself', it is possible to form 'the set of all sets not being a member of themselves', which gives rise to the paradox. Russell, being convinced of the overall correctness of Frege's programme, was not discouraged by it. Broadening the project, Russell believed that all of pure mathematics belonged to logic and set himself the task to demonstrate that this was the case. This was carried out in collaboration with A. N. Whitehead and led to the monumental work *Principia Mathematica* published in 1910–1913.

Coming back to the topic of mathematical philosophy, the quantificational logic is an important tool in one of Russell's most important contributions to analytic philosophy, the theory of descriptions. Put briefly, the theory of descriptions uses logical analysis of propositions to dissolve philosophical problems. To see how it is used consider the statement 'The present king of France is bald'. This statement is intuitively false since there is no king of France. On previous interpretations (the object theory of meaning), though, one could only claim that it is false if one allows that there is a universe of non-empirical objects that contains the king of France. On Russell's interpretation, the problem is dissolved once one finds the statement's correct logical form: it can be reformulated as 'There is an x and x is king of France and x is bald'. Since there is no individual, x, for which 'x is king of France' is true, the statement as a whole is false.[8]

In an early paper, Russell (1901) used the label 'mathematical philosophy' in a broader sense, namely, that philosophy should pay attention to the results and methods of mathematics when solving philosophical problems. Problems may arise because of a confusing conception of a concept. The method is conceptual analysis. A concept that has given rise to numerous puzzles is the 'infinite'. Zeno's paradox, for example, demonstrates that motion is an illusion: for motion to be possible, one has to move across a distance consisting of

---

[7] The extension of a concept, say F, is all objects, a, for which the statement 'a is F' is true. In formal terms it can be interpreted as the collection $\{x : Fx\}$.

[8] I refer to Russell's *Introduction to Mathematical Philosophy* for further details.

an infinite number of parts in a finite amount of time which seems impossible. Russell credits Weierstrass, Dedekind, and Cantor for having found precise definitions of the infinite. Using the new theories of the infinite, the infinitely small and large and sums of infinite sequences, Russell claims, it is possible to find solutions to the philosophical paradoxes. A mathematical solution to Zeno's paradox exploits the fact that infinite sums may converge. The particular sum that is used in Zeno's paradox is $\sum_{i=1}^{\infty}(\frac{1}{2})^i$, that converges to 1.

The infinitely small posed another challenge to mathematicians in the form of infinitesimals until Cauchy introduced the now well-known notion of a limit in the beginning of the nineteenth century. Cauchy further formulated a theory of infinite series drawing the important distinction between a convergent and a divergent series, formulating criteria of convergence and introducing the concept of a radius of convergence. When referring to the infinitely large, Cantor's contributions are most often mentioned: in particular his introduction of cardinal and ordinal numbers. Although many problems concerning the infinite thus found solutions at the turn of the twentieth century, mathematicians and philosophers still discuss the nature of the infinite in a number of contexts. See Easwaran et al. (2023) for an overview. We return to the question of how to characterise the infinitely large at the end of this section.

Before turning to the philosophy of mathematical practice, I note some of the ideas that philosophers of mathematical practice might share with scientific philosophy. The first point concerns the relations between philosophy and mathematics. Russell's advice to collaborate and establish relations between philosophers and mathematicians is still relevant today. Collaborations exist but are rare. Philosophy of mathematical practice further agrees with the scientific philosophers that philosophy should look to recent or relevant parts of mathematics when finding solutions to philosophical problems. Solutions to problems may draw on mathematical results or tools as in Hilbert's version of scientific philosophy. We find examples of this in the following sections. At the same time, we should keep in mind that philosophy and mathematics are two different domains with distinct subject matter and methods. Only in this way is it possible that philosophy can play the role of an equal interlocutor and be a useful guide for mathematics as well as the converse.

The scientific philosopher's guiding principle of 'divide and conquer' fits well with PMP that often asks more specific questions related to the practice of mathematics. One difference between Russell's mathematical philosophy and that of some contemporary philosophers of mathematics consists in the extent of empirical claims or scientific results that can be drawn upon. It is possible to find contemporary philosophers who note that a particular proof is claimed to be beautiful or explanatory and then set themselves the task to formulate a philosophical account of aesthetic judgements that explains the claim. Similarly, a philosopher may draw on cognitive science and theories of perception when explaining how mathematical knowledge is acquired.

Following the scientific philosophers' advice to pay attention to the methods of mathematics, however, does not entail that we have to agree with the particular positions formulated by the scientific or mathematical philosophers. The challenges and concerns of contemporary mathematics are not the same as at the end of the nineteenth century. Indeed, as mathematics develops so do its methods and issues. Most contemporary mathematicians do not seem very interested in the foundations of mathematics as it was conceived around the turn of the nineteenth century. It is, of course, still possible to find mathematicians that are worried about the unrestricted use of the infinite (e.g., using various forms of the axiom of choice), and certain parts of analysis depend on deep set theoretical results. One might also note the recent development of proof assistants that has revived the interest in formal proofs of mathematics (see Avigad (2021)). Besides questions on the foundations of mathematics, a number of other topics are discussed. In light of the growing diversity of mathematical disciplines, one might ask what unifies mathematics. This question was already posed during the twentieth century (Bourbaki 1950) and is still relevant today. Another concern comes from the increased use of computers in mathematics. Besides the use of formal proof checkers, computers have revolutionised how mathematics is done, or at least provided mathematicians with different types of, and in some sense, much stronger tools. Computers are used to experiment (in different senses of the word), to verify (in some cases), to write papers, and to communicate with peers (emails, talks) and to access and store material.

1.2 Philosophy of Mathematical Practice

The label 'philosophy of mathematical practice' has been applied to a number of different approaches to studies of mathematics. The Association for the Philosophy of Mathematical Practice characterises them in the following broad sense:

> Such approaches include the study of a wide variety of issues concerned with the way mathematics is done, evaluated, and applied, and in addition, or in connection therewith, with historical episodes or traditions, applications, educational problems, cognitive questions, etc. We suggest using the label

'philosophy of mathematical practice' as a general term for this gamut of approaches, open to interdisciplinary work.[9]

Typically, though, PMP is characterised in a more restricted way and often not opposed to, but rather as an extension of traditional, or mainstream philosophy of mathematics.[10] For extensive, but quite different accounts, I refer readers to Mancosu (2008a), Van Bendegem (2014) and Giardino (2017). In addition to these three, I recommend the introduction of Ferreirós and Gray (2006) which has a more historical focus. A large and diverse collection of articles can be found in the recent *Handbook of the History and Philosophy of Mathematical Practice*. The editor, Bharath Sriraman, writes in his introduction that 'mathematical practice' intentionally is left undefined so that readers may 'conceptualize it in whatever way they choose to' (Sriraman 2024, p. 4).

An important feature of PMP is that it suggests further questions and topics that can be studied as part of the philosophy of mathematics. In the introduction to the edited volume *The Philosophy of Mathematical Practice*, Paolo Mancosu comments that after Benacerraf's (1973)[11] influential paper, the primary objective of the epistemology of mathematics has become to give an account of how knowledge of abstract mathematical objects is possible. In contrast, the contributors to the same volume wish to *extend* the topics studied under the heading of epistemology. They propose to study visual thinking in mathematics, diagrammatic reasoning, understanding, mathematical explanations, the purity of methods, and mathematical physics. In order to study these topics, they insist that solutions to posed problems require attention to a wide range of mathematical fields. In this sense, Mancosu writes, PMP is both less and more ambitious than mainstream philosophy of mathematics. It is less ambitious since it does not aim to provide solutions to the 'big' problems, such as explaining the nature of mathematical objects, how we acquire knowledge of

---

[9] See the webpage of the Association for the Philosophy of Mathematical Practice: www.philmathpractice.org.

[10] There are a few exceptions. Some philosophers are (still) critical towards mainstream philosophy. One contemporary example is Cellucci (2022) who further claims that PMP as formulated in Mancosu (2008) and Carter (2019) is not radical enough. One might also mention Lakatos' (1976) criticism of the foundational schools as well as Putnam's 'Mathematics without foundations'. Mainstream philosophy of mathematics is described as dealing with questions regarding the ontology of mathematics and topics that are inspired by the classical foundational schools, that is, logicism, intuitionism, and formalism.

[11] Benacerraf's 'Mathematical truth' presents a dilemma for philosophical accounts of mathematics: either we cannot adopt a uniform semantics (for mathematics and our natural language) or we must accept a characterisation of mathematical knowledge that renders it a mystery that we have any knowledge about mathematics at all.

them, and how abstract mathematical entities can tell us anything about the real world. Instead, the philosopher of mathematical practice is more humble and deals with specific questions related to the epistemology of mathematics. It is more ambitious because of the extensive engagement with mathematics that such studies require.

Extending the range of topics that can be discussed under the banner of philosophy entails, as remarked by both Giardino (2017) and Mancosu (2008a), also an appropriate extension of the analytic philosophical toolbox so that it can shed light on the new questions: 'we do not dismiss the analytic tradition in philosophy of mathematics but rather seek to extend its tools to a variety of areas that have been, by and large, ignored' (Mancosu 2008a, p. 18).

Panza (2024) provides some cues about possible components of the extended analytic toolbox. An essential component consists of extracting general features: Although PMP is based on considerations of mathematical practice, as *philosophy* it aims at capturing 'some essential general feature of this practice' (p. 2308–2309). This aspect is what makes philosophy different from history:

> A collection (or system) of case studies cannot but be what it is, namely, a more or less ordered configuration of particular inquiries devoted to single neighborhoods in the space of history. Philosophy is much more and much less than this: It is an account of the space itself. While the former accounts for some elements in a quite large set, the latter defines a structure based on this set and studies it as such. (p. 2310)

Jean Paul Van Bendegem (2014), too, finds that the analytical tradition is present in both PMP and in traditional foundational studies. He suggests to use the formal tools and modelling techniques developed by the analytic tradition to form bridges between studies of mathematical practice and 'traditional' philosophy of mathematics. Van Bendegem points to a few examples of bridges, one in visual thinking: Mumma (2012), discussing a formal system that captures some of the intuitive and constructive characters of Euclidean geometry, forms a bridge between contributions that take as a starting point how diagrams are used in mathematical practice and more formal presentations of Euclidean geometry. (See Section 3 for further details on Euclid's plane geometry.)[12] Formulating such bridges, he argues, is of vital importance to the community of philosophers of mathematical practice:

> I believe the two major tasks for the future are, first, to develop a greater coherence in the field and, two, to keep the conversation going with the other philosophers of mathematics ... These are difficult tasks, no doubt,

---

[12] Arana (2009) is another good example of a bridge. It discusses the use of formal tools to measure the degree of 'purity' of proofs. See Section 1.2.1 for further details on purity.

but … one should not forget that the mainstream in the philosophy of mathematical practice is not mainstream at all in the larger field of the philosophy of mathematics where, for example, foundational studies still form a major part. Setting up the dialogue can, quite frankly, again be a matter of survival. (p. 222)

1.2.1 What Does 'Practice' Mean?

We have noted that PMP introduces new topics in the philosophy of mathematics. Another way to characterise PMP takes as a starting point different interpretations of 'practice' and how they shape which questions are asked and what methods are drawn upon. Carter (2019) describes three main understandings of 'practice' that give rise to different articulations of PMP: agent-based, historical, and epistemological PMP. It is important to note that these strands are not mutually exclusive. Most often more than one of these perspectives are in play.

In the *agent-based* perspective of PMP, 'practice' refers 'mainly to the fact that mathematics is a human activity focussing on the agents, real or idealised, doing mathematics' (Carter 2019, p. 11). Practice thus refers to the different activities associated with doing mathematics. Activities may consist of applying, learning or developing mathematics (Giaquinto, 2005). Focussing on agents' activities might also mean considering mathematics in its cultural, social, and educational contexts as noted by Van Bendegem (2014).

An agent-based perspective might consider general human traits or abilities and how they affect our engagement with mathematics. One might note that human beings have limited visual and cognitive capacities and so what we are able to perceive (and know, perhaps) depends on how information is presented to us. Such an assumption lies behind some of the studies of the role of visual representations that are presented in Section 3. Similar considerations are implicit in the studies of, and comparisons between, the motivations for different notational systems that are used in, for example, logic (see Waszek and Schlimm (2021) and Shin (2002)).

On a broader scale, scholars have objected to the traditional account of mathematical knowledge because it leaves out the role of human agents. Recently, Silvia De Toffoli (2021) has proposed an epistemological framework for mathematics that puts human practitioners at the center of inquiry. On the received view, De Toffoli writes, we acquire knowledge of a mathematical proposition when we have a proof of it, where proof is conceived as a deduction from axioms. That is, knowledge is tied to justification that is obtained via formal proofs.[13] Considered as a description of practice this is too strict. Her first point

---

[13] In philosophy, knowledge is traditionally characterised as 'justified, true belief'.

is that standard proofs in mathematics rarely are in the form of formal proofs. Second, the description leaves out the human dimension, in particular the fact that human beings are fallible. She points to numerous cases where mathematicians thought they had found a proof of a theorem that turned out to contain gaps. One example is Wiles' first proof of Fermat's last theorem. De Toffoli formulates instead what she refers to as a 'fallibilist account of mathematical justification'. This involves the notion of a simil-proof which aspires to model the proofs that mathematicians make, but takes into account that sometimes when formulating arguments and believing they are proofs, they turn out not to be. An argument is a simil-proof 'when it is shareable, and some agents who have judged all its parts to be correct as a result of checking accept it as a proof. Moreover, the argument broadly satisfies the standards of acceptability of the mathematical community to which it is addressed' (p. 835). To be justified in the belief of a proposition then means to be able to come up with a simil-proof for it and be able to appropriately defend this simil-proof.

A few studies provide more detailed descriptions of the notion of a mathematical practice understood as the activities of agents. One is an elaboration of how human activities such as collecting, counting and measuring give rise to abstract mathematical concepts and theories. Mac Lane's *Mathematics: Form and Function* (1986) presents such a picture from a mathematical point of view whereas Ferreirós (2016) has further historical and pragmatic perspectives. A different perspective is offered by Valeria Giardino (2023) who responds to the question 'What is essential to the practice that we call mathematical?'. Her response has two components. One is that mathematics is an activity concerned with conceptual content with an inherent inferential component. The second component emphasises the material tools such as notations and figures used in mathematical reasoning. Giardino combines Brandom's inferentialism with Hutchins' theory of distributed cognition to form what she refers to as *enhanced material inferentialism*.[14]

José Ferreirós (2024) formulates a slightly different characterisation of a practice that emphasises the formulation of abstract mathematical theories and use of material tools in the form of symbolic frameworks. A practice is 'recognized as mathematical due to its links with the notions of number and form (i.e., spatial figures), which may be explicit or implicit; generally speaking, mathematics has to do with the study of patterns, numerical and geometric patterns being prominent' (pp. 2799–2800).

---

[14] Panza (2024) offers a different ontological and epistemic answer to the question 'What is essential to the intellectual activity that we call mathematics?'. Panza argues that it is essential to explain how we can have *de re* epistemic access to the content of mathematics.

A related question is: when is a practice, understood as a human activity, to be counted as a 'mathematical practice' and in which case do such practices give rise to *mathematical* knowledge? Giardino and Ferreirós argue that elementary practices based on basic perception and 'core knowledge systems' that underlie our number sense do not yet constitute mathematical knowledge proper. Ferreirós further discusses whether ethnomathematics is a mathematical practice. According to Ferreirós' characterisation, the activities of ethnomathematics, for example, weaving baskets with intricate mathematical patterns, do not constitute a mathematical practice since they lack both the symbolic framework and the theoretical dimension. Both forms of activities belong to a different level that he refers to as proto-mathematics. It is one of his (see Ferreirós (2016)) points, however, that the theoretical parts of mathematics depend on these lower levels, referring to 'the interplay of practices' or a 'web-of-knowledge'.

Returning to the different strands of mathematical practice, *historical PMP* considers mathematics as the outcome of certain human activities and events. More important is the underlying assumption that mathematics has changed across time and therefore cannot be perceived as a static body of truths. From an historical point of view, one could be interested in the various internal and external factors that influence, and have influenced the development of mathematics over time. The philosopher of mathematical practice might wish to ask if there are any general things to say regarding its development. In the historical PMP, the interconnections between history and philosophy can further be employed for various purposes: Philosophy may offer general categories that help uncover new insights in historical studies (Epple, 2004). Conversely, philosophical questions may be investigated by analysing historical case studies.

Historical perspectives may enrich a philosophical study by revealing sources of ideas and by suggesting new categories and different interpretations. To illustrate how, we give an example concerning the phenomenon 'reverse mathematics'. In contemporary mathematical logic 'reverse mathematics' refers to the program of Harvey Friedman and Stephen Simpson (see, e.g., Simpson (2009)). The point is to determine which set existence axioms are needed to prove particular mathematical results. They have formulated a hierarchy of logical subsystems that have been used to determine the strength of major results from all parts of mathematics, including logic, arithmetic, analysis and algebra. The fundamental idea when determining the strength of a proposition is that one does not only prove that the proposition follows from a particular subsystem – one also proves that the subsystem can be derived from the proposition (modulo the base system in which reasoning takes place).

In this way, it is certain that the subsystem is the weakest possible system in which the result is provable.

Taking an historical perspective reveals that the idea of asking which axioms are needed to prove a particular proposition is not a recent invention. Victor Pambuccian (2009) traces it back to the ancient Greeks, more precisely to Pappus of Alexandria, and refers to it as 'reverse geometry' (see also Arana (2008)). It further appears in Hilbert's *Foundations of Geometry*. At the end of this work, Hilbert ties attempts at proving impossibility results to what he refers to as the 'purity' of methods in demonstration and writes: 'the preceding geometrical study attempts ... to explain what are the axioms, hypotheses, or means necessary to the demonstration of a truth of elementary geometry' (Hilbert 1950, p. 82).

Andrew Arana (2008, 2022) further argues that different concerns seem to be at stake when mathematicians ask for which axioms are necessary to prove a particular result. Friedman and Simpson's reverse mathematics uses tools from proof theory and computability theory to analyse the computational or combinatorial content of mathematical theorems, which Arana (2008, p. 37) refers to as 'strong logical purity'. In contrast, one may search for the 'right, proper, essential, or appropriate' axioms (2022, p. 403). Arana ties the latter to Aristotle's concern of finding definitions that reveal the essence of a thing, which further entails that definitions, or axioms, cannot introduce 'foreign elements': a definition of a concept in number theory, for example, cannot rely on geometry.

Second, historical studies might throw light on why certain philosophical programs such as the foundational schools were initiated. Such studies do not at the outset belong to philosophy. But awareness of the historical circumstances under which a program or text has been produced might affect how it is interpreted. Tappenden (2006) is a good example illustrating how this is the case in some of Frege's writings. James Tappenden claims that Frege has often been interpreted from a narrow and distorted point of view and, if one reads him according to his contemporary mathematical background, a different and richer picture emerges. Tappenden considers the following passage:

> *Proof is now demanded of many things that formerly passed as self-evident.* Again and again the limits to the validity of a proposition have been established for the first time. The concepts of function, of continuity, of limit, and of infinity have been shown to stand in need of a sharper definition ... *In all directions the same ideals can be seen at work – rigor of proof,* precise delimitation of extent of validity, and as a means to this, sharp definition of concepts. [FA 1884, p. 1] (Tappenden, p. 118, my italics)

On a formalist reading, one might wish to emphasise the passages in italics and claim that Frege's main concerns were the validity of propositions and rigorous proofs. If one reads the passage bearing in mind the state of affairs in Frege's mathematical field, one could instead focus on the other issues mentioned: how to define fundamental concepts and determine the domain of application of central principles. Tappenden tells us that Frege's field was geometry and complex analysis from a Riemannian perspective. This field was in wild disarray in the second half of the nineteenth century. There was a dispute about Weierstrass' computational and Riemann's conceptual approaches (see Stein (1988)). One disagreement concerned how to define a complex function. Riemann's conceptual approach defined a complex function by the today well-known Cauchy–Riemann equations, that is, in terms of a given property. Weierstrass believed that the proper way to treat complex functions was by their power series or as analytic expressions and to calculate. Today we know that these two characterisations are essentially co-extensive. But this fact was not known before 1900. Another concern was the domain of application of various principles. One fundamental result is Dirichlet's principle, which establishes the existence of certain functions under given conditions. It was used, for example, in Riemann's famous work on Abelian functions to establish the existence of functions on a Riemann surface of genus g with poles at specified points. It turned out that Dirichlet's principle was used in cases where it did not hold. A precise formulation and a rigorous proof were given by Hilbert in 1901. It may be some of these concerns that Frege refers to when he writes that '[t]he concepts of function, of continuity, of limit, and of infinity have been shown to stand in need of a sharper definition' and that 'the same ideals can be seen at work – rigor of proof, precise delimitation of extent of validity, and as a means to this, sharp definition of concepts'.

The final approach, *epistemological* PMP, considers 'practice' in a more abstract or general way, referring to mathematics itself, or the many ways that it is presented or accessible to human beings. In this case, 'practice' may refer to mathematical results or theories as presented in articles, books, at talks, and so on, or what mathematicians themselves say or write about mathematics. The requirement in this strand is that whatever philosophical question is asked, we need to consider the relevant part of mathematics in order to respond to it.

As part of epistemological PMP, philosophers are examining how to capture what mathematicians might mean when they say that a result is deep or a proof is explanatory. A special issue has been devoted to different characterisations of depth in mathematics (*Philosophia Mathematica*, Volume 23 (2), published in 2015). One may also consider qualities from an abstract point of view and discuss the general notion of virtues in mathematics, see Aberdein et al. (2021).

The topic of 'mathematical explanations' has received much attention. When referring to 'explanations' in mathematics it is useful to distinguish between an external and an internal point of view (Mancosu 2008b). The external perspective discusses whether mathematical facts can serve as explanations in other domains and the implications this has for the ontology of mathematics. Philosophers also consider explanations that are internal to mathematics, in particular how to characterise explanatory proofs. Two main proposals (Steiner (1978) and Kitcher (1984)) have been critically examined.[15] Steiner defends the view that an explanatory proof makes evident how a characterising property of an entity mentioned in the proposition leads to the conclusion.[16] Kitcher characterises explanations in terms of a notion of unification. Others have suggested modifications to these views (see, for example, Lange (2018)). I refer to Mancosu et al. (2023) for further details as well as an overview on the topic of mathematical explanations. One might also take a broader perspective and consider explanations in mathematics, not only in connection with proofs, but also as related to mathematical understanding (see Carter (forthcoming)).

The last example of epistemological PMP returns to the much discussed concept, the infinite. This example further illustrates that typically many different aspects of practice such as historical case studies or results from contemporary mathematics are involved in PMP studies. The example is based on a forthcoming contribution by Mancosu (forthcoming). Mancosu discusses, among other things, an interpretation of the infinitely large formulated by the medieval scholar Robert Grosseteste (ca 1168–1253) and – using recent results from measure theory – argues that Grosseteste's idea can be made mathematically rigorous. Today, the standard conception of the size, or cardinality of a set, states that two sets have the same size if their elements can be brought in a one-one correspondence.[17] Grosseteste, an Oxford theologian, had a different intuition. According to this conception, if two infinite collections A, B fulfil that $A \subsetneq B$, then the size of A is strictly less than the size of B. Mancosu refers to some passages of Grosseteste's work *Commentary on the Physics* where he proposes certain ideas concerning measuring the number of points of finite line segments. The basic idea is that we choose a specific line segment as our unit and that it will contain a given number of points. (According to Grosseteste, whereas human beings can only measure line segments relative to a unit, God assigns an absolute infinite number to the number of points of the unit segment.) The unit line segment is used as a 'measure', that is, any other (finite) line segment can be measured relative to it. The idea includes a number of

---

[15] See, for example, Hafner and Mancosu (2005, 2008), and Tappenden (2005).

[16] A characterising property of an entity is one that singles this entity out in a domain of similar entities.

[17] A different way to say that two sets M, N have the same cardinality is that there exists a one-to-one and onto function $f: M \to N$.

assumptions: If two line segments have equal lengths, then they contain the same number of points. If the length of a line segment is a rational number times the unit line, then their numbers of points are also in the same proportion.

Grosseteste's ideas, as Mancosu points out, were challenged by later scholars. One is Fishacre (1205–1248) whose most famous challenge was a demonstration that there is a one-one correspondence between any two finite line segments. Although Fishacre is mostly unknown today, the ensuing discussion influenced other thinkers such as Oresme and Galileo (see Mancosu (forthcoming) for details).

Mancosu demonstrates how tools from measure theory and the notion of an elementary numerosity (that counts the number of points of a line segment) can be used to implement Grosseteste's idea. Grosseteste's conception of the measurement of finite line segments and their corresponding number of points, assumes that there is a correlation between the measure of the finite segments and the numerosities of points they contain. Mancosu refers to Benci, Bottazzi, and Di Nasso (2015) who show that if L is the Lebesgue measure on $\mathbb{R}$, then it is possible to construct an elementary numerosity on $\mathbb{R}$ that has the desired properties: Finite line segments of equal length have exactly the same (infinite) numerosity of points. This concludes the summary of the relevant sections of Mancosu's forthcoming book.

Based on the different interpretations of practice, it might appear as if the philosophy of mathematical practice consists of a number of diverse and incompatible approaches. Carter (2019) suggests this need not be the case and presents a simple overall framework to capture the various approaches to PMP. It consists of two components, *mathematics* and *agents*.[18] The component 'mathematics' contains the part of mathematics that is considered, for example, theories, concepts, propositions, axioms, proofs, and so on. The second component refers to the human agents, real or idealised and their mathematical activities. The idea is that philosophical studies considers variations of these two components as well as relations between them. The strands presented earlier emphasise different aspects of mathematical practice and so will take different starting points: whereas the agent-based strand's main focus is on the human agents and how, for example, mathematical knowledge is shaped through their 'practices', the starting point of the epistemological strand is mathematics itself – sometimes leaving out considerations of agents completely. The historical strand primarily focuses on examining the interplay

---

[18] Ferreirós (2016) presents a similar practice matrix with two components consisting of 'framework' and 'agents'.

between mathematics, its concepts, theorems, theories, and so on, and the practices (of human agents) that shape its development.

2 Structure in Mathematics

One way to conceive of the philosophy of mathematical practice is that it focuses on mathematics as an activity and the questions that arise from this point of view. Rather than considering mathematics as a body of truths and discussing the nature of its objects (including how we gain access to them), the philosophy of mathematical practice (PMP) may discuss questions related to how concepts are shaped and theories relate to each other, which methods are used, and so on. In this sense we are interested in understanding what mathematics is from a broader perspective than just what mathematics is about.

In the light of this, we will consider mathematical structuralism from the point of view of how mathematics is done rather than discussing the nature of structures. The latter approach is most often taken in mainstream philosophy of mathematics. Indeed, philosophical structuralism has its roots in a famous article by P. Benacerraf (1965) that discusses the nature of the natural numbers. Benacerraf objected to the set theoretic reductions of the natural numbers, instead emphasising its structural features.[19] The characterisation of structures and their nature has since become an important topic in the philosophy of mathematics.

We focus on different types of relations in mathematics – both from a local and a global point of view – and some of the roles they play. Locally, in the sense that mathematics studies structures, that can be characterised in terms of relations between objects, rather than properties of, say, quantities. From a global point of view, I emphasise the importance of formal relations between structures but also the exploitation of relations in a much broader sense. The content of this section is as follows. Section 2.1 presents a few preliminaries and general details about mathematical structuralism. Section 2.2 sketches the development of some central components of a structuralist view of mathematics. This sketch centres around the use of the axiomatic method as a tool to create individual structures but it can also be seen as a way to organise or 'structure' mathematical theories, or even mathematics as a whole. We present the axiomatic method as formulated in David Hilbert's writings. A similar method can be found in the Peano school and both are supposedly inspired by Hermann Grassmann (Cantù 2020). The method, as we will see, is later used and modified by Emmy Noether and Nicolas Bourbaki.

---

[19] Structural views of mathematics can be traced back even further, see Reck and Schiemer (2020).

Another topic concerns the emergence and awareness of the importance of structures in mathematics, from Hilbert's formulation of axioms that characterise relations between entities to the freestanding algebraic structures introduced by Noether.

The last component to be mentioned is the focus on relations, not only between objects or places in a particular structure, but on a global scale. We find this idea in Noether's work, for example, in her formulation of the isomorphism theorems that establish relations between structures and certain substructures. The idea is later further developed and formalised in category theory, for example, by the notion of a functor.

This brief historical sketch complements the one that is given in Shapiro and Hellman (2018) which focuses, in particular, on the emergence of a structural view of geometry. Broader perspectives can be found in Corry (2004), Krömer (2007), and Reck and Schiemer (2020). Corry's *Modern Algebra and the Rise of Mathematical Structures* gives a detailed account of the history of algebra from around 1850 to the rise of category theory. Krömer's *Tool and Object* is a rich introduction to the recent history of category theory including a discussion about some of its structuralist themes. *The Pre-history of Mathematical Structuralism* edited by Reck and Schiemer contains chapters that explore structural views of both mathematicians and philosophers from the nineteenth century until the early twentieth century, ranging from H. Grassmann and C. S. Peirce to S. Mac Lane and W. V. O. Quine. For a general introduction to 'mathematical structuralism' I refer to Reck and Schiemer (2023).

Finally, in Section 2.3, I focus on the role of global relations in mathematics and illustrate that relations of various kinds play a role when we determine properties of objects in mathematics.

2.1 Structuralism in Philosophy

Structures undeniably play an essential role in modern mathematics, making a structuralist view of mathematics well aligned with mathematical practice. Today mathematics is comprised of a vast number of fields, each studying its particular types of structure, for example, vector spaces in linear algebra, topological spaces in topology, manifolds in differential geometry, and various types of spaces such as Banach spaces in functional analysis. Furthermore, as stressed by Mac Lane (1986) these entities are studied by forming relations to other types of structures, for example, by associating algebraic structures such as groups to topological spaces as is done in algebraic topology or establishing programs such as the Langlands' program that systematically exploits links between domains. These developments have both inspired and, in some cases, been strengthened by the development of category theory, which, through the notions of functors and natural transformations, formalises the use of global relations in mathematics.[20]

According to mathematical structuralism, contemporary mathematics can be characterised as the science of (abstract) structures. Alternatively, one might say that mathematics focuses on relations rather than intrinsic properties of objects. From this it has been inferred that mathematical objects only have structural properties, that is, properties that follow from the relations that define the structure in which they have a place.

A structure can be characterised in different ways. One might think of a structure as a collection of objects on which there is defined a number of relations. Another way is to say that mathematics studies systems of objects that are defined by a collection of axioms and that these axioms characterise relations between the objects. There might be multiple systems of objects satisfying the axioms (that is, models) but they will be considered as isomorphic (with respect to the particular structure). The structure is then said to be defined 'up to isomorphism'. This feature is sometimes characterised by the slogan that mathematics studies 'one over many'.

A simple and often referred to example is the natural numbers. What characterises the set of natural numbers from a structuralist point of view is its structure as a progression, that is, the natural numbers consists of a certain countable collection on which there is defined an order relation and it has an initial object under this relation. One might also refer to the Dedekind–Peano axioms and characterise the natural numbers as the structure that has an initial object and a successor function (obeying certain properties). In both cases, the particular numbers do not have any individuating properties other than those that follow from this characterisation. The number 1, for example, is nothing but the second place in the natural number structure, or the successor of the initial object (assuming that the initial object is zero). From another point of view, one might want to consider the natural numbers together with the operations of addition and multiplication and say that they form, for example, the positive cone of the ring of integers.

Other typical examples include the algebraic structures, for example, groups or fields. In this case the axioms of a group, say, characterise the group

---

[20] Category theory has also been used to formulate formal foundations in mathematics. The Elementary Theory of the Category of Sets and the more recent Homotopy Type Theory are examples of this. Category theory has also inspired a number of structuralist accounts of mathematics. I refer readers to Landry and Marquis (2005) and Reck and Schiemer (2023).

structure.[21] From this perspective no element of a group – except the neutral element – can be individuated. Elements only have properties that follow from the axioms, for example, that every element has a unique inverse. Notice the difference between the two examples: In the first example, the Dedekind–Peano axioms intend to define a particular structure, the natural numbers. We say that the axioms are categorical (or non-algebraic). In the second case, referring to algebraic structures, the axioms are non-categorical in the sense that many different collections fulfil the group axioms. Examples of groups include the integers with addition or invertible $n \times n$ matrices with complex numbers as entries under multiplication, denoted as $(GL_n(\mathbb{C}), \cdot)$. Considered as individual collections, groups might have additional properties: The integers, for example, is an abelian group whereas $(GL_n(\mathbb{C}), \cdot)$ is not.

2.2 Emergence of Structures

Mathematical structuralism as a philosophical position is inspired by the general historical development of mathematics: observing that it has changed from studying properties of quantities and space to the structured systems – the objects of modern mathematics. The account given here begins with Hilbert at the turn of the twentieth century, but proto-structuralist ideas existed earlier (see the introduction of Reck and Schiemer (2020)): One might mention the growing importance of a set-theoretic perspective in mathematics. Cantor and Dedekind are usually mentioned as the fathers of set theory, but both find inspiration in the work of Riemann (Ferreirós 2007). In addition, there is the awareness of the limitations of the previous theories of logic in capturing mathematical reasoning, and so a number of scholars undertook the task of developing new versions of logic, or formal tools. Besides the well-known Frege and Russell mentioned in Section 1, there are also Boole, De Morgan, Schröder and Peirce. De Morgan and Peirce even formulated different versions of a logic of relations. Finally there is the recognition that mathematics is not anymore simply the science of numbers and geometry but instead a study of relations.

2.2.1 Hilbert on the Axiomatic Method

Bourbaki (1950) stresses the importance of the axiomatic method as a component of structuralism and elsewhere attributes it to David Hilbert (1862–1943).

---

[21] A group, $(G, \circ)$ is defined as a set, G, on which there is defined a closed operation $\circ \colon G \times G \to G$ that fulfils the following axioms: (i) For any $a, b, c \in G$, $a \circ (b \circ c) = (a \circ b) \circ c$, (ii) there exists a neutral element $e \in G$ such that $a \circ e = e \circ a = a$ for all $a \in G$, and (iii) For all $a \in G$ there exists an inverse a^{-1} for which $a \circ a^{-1} = a^{-1} \circ a = e$.

In the philosophy of mathematics, Hilbert is mainly known for his later work on the foundations of mathematics, as the founder of formalism. As part of this programme Hilbert created proof theory with the intent to give a finitist proof of the consistency of mathematics. He was, however, concerned with the foundations of mathematics throughout his career when he conceived and tackled questions regarding foundations in different ways. Sieg (2020) explains that Hilbert's contributions to the foundations of mathematics can be characterised in two main ways: The first involves a structural axiomatic approach, while the second is based on proof theory and formal methods. In the late nineteenth century, thinking about the foundations of arithmetic, Hilbert was influenced by Dedekind's logicist views. By 1904 Hilbert expressed that the consistency of the axioms of arithmetic would be demonstrated if one could show that no contradictions could be derived from the axioms. Sieg refers to this as a 'quasi-syntactic' view, since the idea of a formal system including deduction rules had not yet been developed. It was only after 1917 that Hilbert began to develop his meta-mathematics. This came after studies of Whitehead and Russell's *Principia Mathematica* and a realisation that the underlying principles of *reasoning* had to be spelled out in order to formulate a foundation for mathematics (using mathematical tools as pointed out in the previous section). By principles of reasoning, I refer to both the basic (logical) assumptions as well as the inference rules. In this way reasoning becomes a calculus and the rules and assumptions can be studied by mathematical tools.

Hilbert formulated the axiomatic method during his earlier work on the foundations of mathematics and as part of the structural axiomatic approach. It is explicitly addressed in Hilbert's 'Axiomatic thought' (1918) but he uses the basic ideas much earlier in his *Grundlagen der Geometrie* which was first published in 1899. In the rest of this section, I refer to the English title, *Foundations of Geometry* (*FoG*). The *Foundations of Geometry* has its roots in the plane geometry of Euclid's *Elements* and its axiomatic presentation. Some of the more recent developments of geometry are added and it is presented in a form where all assumptions are spelled out. Concerning assumptions, it was long since known that the *Elements* drew on certain assumptions that were not included among the axioms. Already the first proposition of book I reads off information from the accompanying diagram, that is, that two circles intersect in a point (see Section 3 for further details).[22] The missing assumption in this

---

[22] The first proposition tells us how to construct an equilateral triangle on a given line segment. Given line segment AB the construction begins by drawing two circles with radius AB. One circle with centre in A, the other in B. Postulate 3 tells us we can do this. In the next step one observes that the two circles intersect in a point C. But none of the definitions, postulates or common notions grant its existence.

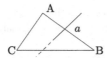

Figure 1 Pasch's axiom: Let A, B, C be three points that do not lie on a line and let a be a line in the plane ABC which does not meet any of the points A, B, C. If the line a passes through a point of the segment AB, it also passes through a point of the segment AC, or through a point of segment BC (Hilbert 1950, p. 5).

case is an axiom of contnuity. The fourth proposition states that if two triangles have an angle in common and the two line segments that enclose the angles are pairwise equal then the two other angles and remaining line segments will also be pairwise equal. The demonstration superimposes the two triangles and so exploits that properties are not changed when a geometric figure is placed at a different location. Further assumptions were identified and spelled out in the nineteenth century by Pasch (1882/1926) in his *Vorlesungen uber neuere Geometrie*. The axiom that is now named after him states that if a line passes one side in a triangle, then, if continued, it will eventually go through one of the other two sides; see Figure 1. The non-Euclidean geometry that was formulated by Gauss, Bolyai and Lobachevsky during the first half of the nineteenth century is included in the *FoG*, as is the projective geometry developed by Desargues and later Poncelet, among others.

Another major difference between Euclid's *Elements* and Hilbert's geometry concerns the content of the axioms. Book I of the *Elements* starts out by defining all considered geometrical objects, a point, line segment, circle, and so on, and some of their properties. The postulates (except number IV) tell us which constructions are permissible under given configurations of points and line segments. In this way, further points, lines and geometric figures are constructed as we work our way through the propositions. Each proposition starts out with certain given geometric objects, for example, a line segment (and so also its endpoints). By systematically using the postulates further geometric objects appear (Panza 2012). In contrast, there are no definitions of the basic geometric objects in Hilbert's geometry. He does not say what a point, line or plane is; Hilbert assumes the 'three distinct systems of things' exist and gives them different labels according to the category they belong to. The purpose of the listed axioms is then to tell us how the elements of the three systems are *related*:

> We think of these points, straight lines, and planes as having certain mutual relations, which we indicate by means of such words as "are situated", "between", "parallel", "congruent", "continuous", etc. The complete and

exact description of these relations follows as a consequence of the *axioms of geometry*. (Hilbert 1950, p. 2, italics in original)

The axioms are presented in five different groups. The groups consist of axioms of connection, order (defining the relation 'between' on points on line segments), parallels (containing the parallel postulate), congruence, and continuity.[23] The first group of axioms characterises the relations between the system of things, that is, the points, lines and planes. The axioms tell us, for example, that two distinct points determine a line and conversely that two lines determine a point.[24] Other groups include axioms that were drawn upon in Euclid's *Elements* but not explicitly mentioned such as the beforementioned axiom of continuity. The axioms of congruence enable a proof of a proposition corresponding to the beforementioned proposition I.4.

The presentation in the *Foundations of Geometry* has certain structural implications. The first is that we can deal only with objects to the degree that they are 'fixed' by the relations defined on the system. A point, for example, has no intrinsic properties, it can only be determined as the point of intersection between two lines. The second is that a group of axioms together characterises a given structure, or theory (in this case a geometry). Third, the axioms do not come with a fixed ontology: the theory applies to any system of objects that fulfils the axioms. This is often illustrated by Hilbert's famous quote: 'one must be able to say "tables, chairs, beer-mugs" each time in place of "points, lines, planes"' which Hilbert allegedly said to Otto Blumenthal at the Berlin train station in 1891.

Around the same time as Hilbert published the *Foundations of Geometry*, he wrote the short article 'Über den Zahlbegriff' (1900) where he notes that the axiomatic method is also the right method to use when one wishes to study the logical foundation of other areas than geometry – including arithmetic. The article presents the axioms for the real numbers in a similar way as in the *Foundations of Geometry*, that is, as belonging to different groups: axioms of connection, calculations (commutative associative and distributive laws), order and continuity of the numbers. In brief, together they characterise the real numbers as a complete, ordered field that fulfils the Archimedean principle. Later the axiomatic method is applied to all of mathematics. In 'Axiomatic thought', the method and all its advantages are spelled out, mentioning numerous

---

[23] The groups of axioms are presented in different orders in later versions of the book where Hilbert explores the conclusions obtainable from different combinations of them.

[24] The axioms are *Two distinct points A and B always determine a straight line a. We write that AB = a or BA = a* and axiom two is *Any two distinct points of a straight line completely determine that line; that is, if AB = a and AC = a, where B ≠ C, then is also BC = a.*

examples from both mathematics and physics, including set theory, thermo-dynamics and mechanics.

The aim of formulating mathematics on an axiomatic framework is connected with Hilbert's concerns with the foundations of mathematics. In the introduction to the *FoG*, certain now familiar foundational concepts are explicitly mentioned:

> The following investigation is a new attempt to choose for geometry a *simple* and *complete* set of *independent* axioms and to deduce from these the most important geometrical theorems in such a manner as to bring out as clearly as possible the significance of the different groups of axioms and the scope of the conclusions to be derived from the individual axioms. (Hilbert 1950, p. 1, italics in original)

One purpose is therefore to offer (groups of) axioms that are mutually independent and complete. Corry (2006) points out that by 'complete' Hilbert at this time intends a pragmatic notion, that is, the aim is that all known results of geometry should be possible to prove. The intention is not that all possible 'true' results of geometry are provable (thus avoiding the consequence of Gödel's first incompleteness theorem that was published later in 1931). These aims are also mentioned in his 'Über den Zahlbegriff' as well as in his later 'Axiomatic thought'. But note also the last sentence in the quote that mentions a different aim, that of 'exploring the significance and consequences of the different groups of axioms'. This is related to the progressive part of the axiomatic method (Hilbert 1918, paragraph 6)

> [T]he progressive development of the individual field of knowledge then lies solely in the further logical construction of the already mentioned framework of concepts.

In addition to simply deriving consequences from the formulated axioms of a theory, Hilbert emphasises the fruitfulness of the method. Several paragraphs of 'Axiomatic thought' are devoted to explaining how a deepening of the foundations and exploring the dependence and independence of propositions lead to new results. Hilbert mentions examples from mathematics as well as physics. One obvious example is the independence of the parallel postulate which led to the construction of entirely new geometries.

Besides the fact that axioms define relations and that a group of axioms characterises a structure, a different interpretation of 'structure' arises from the axiomatic method. It concerns how one chooses to build – or structure – a particular theory, that is, which principles are chosen as one's axioms or first principles. In this case, one might refer to the logical structure of a theory.

The logical structure of a theory is mentioned in the beginning of 'Axiomatic thought' using words like 'order' and 'logical relations':

> When we assemble the facts of a definite, more-or-less comprehensive field of knowledge, we soon notice that these facts are capable of being ordered. ... a concept of this framework corresponds to each individual object of the field of knowledge, and a logical relation between concepts corresponds to every fact within the field of knowledge. (pp. 1107–1108)

In this way mathematical theories are organised in terms of their logical structure. In Bourbaki (1950) we find a different way to organise mathematics that we turn to later in this section.

How to structure – or present – a theory becomes relevant as a consequence of a change in the conception of the status of axioms. One might hold that an axiom is a 'true' characterisation of the mathematical subject matter or that the purpose of axioms is to reveal the essence of the characterised concepts. After the publication of Hilbert's *Foundations of Geometry* a famous correspondence followed between Hilbert and Frege debating the nature and role of axioms. (Frege further criticised the lack of definitions fixing the meaning of concepts in the *FoG*.) Frege defended the view that axioms are true and that it therefore was not necessary to prove that groups of axioms are consistent. Hilbert, on the other hand, responded – with the much discussed claim – that

> if the arbitrarily given axioms do not contradict each other with all their consequences, then they are true and the things defined by them exist. This is for me the criterion of truth and existence. (Hellman & Shapiro 2018, p. 23)

Other contemporary writers tended to agree with Hilbert's view that axioms should not be considered as true, but merely hypothetical, as suppositions from which to reason. I refer to Feferman (1999), Schlimm (2013) and Cantù (2022) for different roles of axioms in mathematics and to Hellman and Shapiro (2018) on the Hilbert–Frege correspondence.

2.2.2 Noether and Algebraic Structures

Emmy Noether introduced axioms that characterise abstract algebraic structures such as rings and ideals which become 'freestanding' mathematical structures. One might claim that Hilbert's structures also are freestanding in the sense that they apply to any collection of objects fulfilling the relations formulated by the axioms.[25] But the structures mentioned are intended to characterise

---

[25] Hilbert exploits that axioms apply to different domains when he demonstrates the relative consistency and independence of the various (groups of) axioms. To show the consistency of all

a specific field or domain, for example, geometry or the real numbers. Noether's algebraic structures are truly general or non-categorical. In Noether's work we also find the emergence of further structuralist themes that are characteristic for contemporary mathematics. She formulates what is referred to as structure theorems and establishes formal relations between structures. It is also important to notice the influence Noether had through her students and other mathematicians that she talked to. Her student van der Waerden mentions her as a main source of inspiration in his influential textbook *Moderne Algebra*. She also promoted the use of algebraic invariants which contributed to the development of algebraic topology and had an impact on Mac Lane, who, together with Eilenberg, later developed category theory (McLarty 2006).

Noether, born in 1882 in Erlangen, was the daughter of Max Noether, professor in mathematics there. Max Noether was a colleague of Paul Gordan, who would become Noether's doctoral advisor, and a friend of Klein and Hilbert, both located in Göttingen. In 1915 Hilbert and Klein invited Emmy Noether to come to Göttingen to work on invariant theory. From 1919 she started her work on algebra which is the area most often mentioned in connection with her contributions to a structuralist view of mathematics. She was invited to work at Bryn Mawr College in the US in 1933 and died in Princeton in 1935.

Noether (1921, 1927) wrote two influentual papers on algebra, the first, 'Idealtheorie in Ringbereichen', the second, 'Abstrakter Aufbau der Idealtheorie in algebraischen Zahl- und Funktionenkörpern'. Both appeared in the Mathematische Annalen. In the first of these articles Noether proves a generalised version of the fundamental theorem of arithmetic, more precisely that an ideal of a module (or ring) can be written uniquely as a product of prime ideals. A major accomplishment is that she identifies precisely which assumptions are required to prove this result. In addition to the axioms of a ring, the proof requires the ascending chain condition which is an original contribution by Noether. A ring fulfilling this condition is today called a Noetherian ring.

Besides ideals and rings, the algebraic structures of a field and group were already known by the time Noether wrote her papers. What is new to her approach is, firstly, that she considers the algebraic structures as abstract entities where, before, they were thought of as generalisations of the various number domains. Because of this, rings or fields were implicitly assumed to have properties that these domains shared. By considering them as abstract entities in their own right, Noether was able to identify all assumptions needed

---

groups of axioms, for example, he constructs a model consisting of a domain of algebraic numbers.

to prove the considered results. Van der Waerden (1935) later characterised her style saying that

> Any relationships between numbers, functions and operations only become clear, generally applicable, and fully productive after they have been isolated from their particular objects and been formulated as universally valid concepts . . . She was unable to grasp any theorem, any argument unless it had been made abstract and thus made transparent to the eye of her mind. (p. 101)

Algebra has its roots in computations and solving equations. Solutions to the cubic and quartic equations were found during the sixteenth century and collected in Cardano's *Ars Magna* (published in 1545). These accomplishments were followed by a desire to find similar solutions to the quintic which turned out not to be possible. Following methods set out by Lagrange, Abel and Galois were able to demonstrate the insolubility of polynomial equations of a degree higher than four. Two of the fundamental concepts that came from these studies are permutation groups and polynomials over a field. Problems in number theory also led to advances in algebra. The most famous problem is Fermat's last theorem; another influential result was that of 'the law of quadratic reciprocity' formulated by Euler while working on results of Fermat. In the simplest form, this asks which primes, p, can be written as a square modulo another prime q. The surprising fact is that if p, q are odd primes, $p \neq q$ and either p or q is equal to 1 modulo 4, then p is a square mod q if and only if q is a square mod p. Gauss's work on higher reciprocity laws led him to introduce the Gaussian integers, $\mathbb{Z}[\sqrt{-1}]$, which are numbers of the form $a + b \cdot \sqrt{-1}$ for a and b integers. A generalisation of such numbers includes numbers of the form $a + b\sqrt{-n}$, for n square free.

  While considering these different number domains it became clear that the usual properties of the integers do not always hold. An important property, stated in the fundamental theorem of arithmetic, is that any number can be uniquely decomposed as a product of prime numbers. An example of a ring where this is not true is $\mathbb{Z}[\sqrt{-5}]$. In this ring it is possible to write, for example, 6 as a product of irreducible factors in two ways: $3 \cdot 2 = (1 + \sqrt{-5})(1 - \sqrt{-5})$. The numbers, 2, 3 and $1 \pm \sqrt{-5}$ can all be shown to be irreducible in $\mathbb{Z}[\sqrt{-5}]$. To restore this property, Kummer, Kronecker and later Dedekind introduced notions that grew into the concepts of an ideal and a prime ideal. Dedekind's definition of an ideal is essentially the one that is used today and it is Dedekind's work that was the starting point of Noether's contributions to algebra.[26]

---

[26] As one of the editors of Dedekind's collected works, Noether knew his contributions well. She famously kept saying about her own contributions that 'Es steht alles in Dedekind', that is,

Noether's *Idealtheorie in Ringbereichen* formulates first the conditions that define a commutative ring and ideals in such a ring. Noether only considers finitely generated ideals and proves that the ascending chain condition (a.c.c.) follows.[27] She also notes that if one assumes the a.c.c., then ideals of a given ring will be finitely generated and consequently that one may assume the a.c.c. condition instead. In other words, these two conditions are equivalent over the axioms of a commutative ring.

Noether defines a commutative ring as a system of things fulfilling six axioms quite similar to how it is defined today. The first axioms assert the commutativity and associativity of addition and multiplication and the distributive law. The last axiom, called the unlimited and uniqueness of subtraction, states that for any two elements a, b in the ring, there exists a unique element x that solves the equation $a+x = b$. The existence and uniqueness of a zero-object follow from the last axiom. The main result, the unique decomposition of ideals, states that any two decompositions will contain the same number of primary ideals, in Noether's words:

Theorem IX Given two different shortest representations of an ideal as the least common multiple of primary ideals, the number of components will be the same.[28]

The decomposition of ideals into prime ideals is an example of what is referred to as a 'structure theorem', that is, a theorem that tells us how a type of structure can be decomposed into simpler objects. The basic idea of such theorems is that a particular object can be written (uniquely) as, for example, a product or direct sum of certain basic building blocks (primes, prime ideals, etc.).

As mentioned, Noether carefully chooses her axioms so that they suffice to prove the unique decomposition of ideals. The approach of searching for just the right, or minimal, axioms required to prove a given result is seen to a greater extent in her 1927 paper where she also explores which conclusions are obtainable from given groups of axioms. It has been suggested that her style and the concern of finding the 'right' axioms are inspired by Dedekind

---

that her results can be found in the writings of Dedekind. McLarty (2017) suggests we take her statement with a grain of salt – or perhaps that it should be read as Noether bragging about her accomplishments: She was able to see what Dedekind had missed.

[27] The a.c.c. is formulated as follows. If given an ascending chain of ideals, that is, $I_1 \subseteq I_2 \subseteq I_3 \ldots$, there exists a maximal ideal I_k such that for all $k \geq n$, $I_n = I_k$.

[28] The result is shown in a number of steps. She proves first – using the a.c.c. – that any ideal is decomposable as an intersection of a finite number of primary ideals. This theorem is a combination of the fact that any ideal can be decomposed as the intersection of a finite number of irreducible ideals (Th. II) and the fact that any irreducible ideal is primary. (Th VI).

(McLarty 2017).[29] In addition, her approach can be seen as an application of Hilbert's axiomatic method, an instance of what he refers to as 'deepening of foundations'.[30]

The final structural theme, namely, the formulation of formal relations *between* structures emerges, for example, in the shape of the isomorphism theorems found in Noether's 1927 paper. These theorems establish that certain abstract relations exist between structures and certain specified subsets and constructions on them (equivalence classes). Furthermore, these relations are expressed without mentioning any elements of the structures or the operations defined on them.

The theorems are formulated in the context of modules and later in the setting of ideals of a ring, $\mathcal{R}$. The section begins with a definition stating that two $\mathcal{R}$-modules, M and $\bar{M}$, are homomorphic when there is a function from M to $\bar{M}$ that preserves the operations on elements. If the map is bijective, it is an isomorphism in which case M and $\bar{M}$ are said to be isomorphic. Noether then introduces congruence classes and formulates the homomorphism theorem (which is sometimes today referred to as the first isomorphism theorem). The theorem states that if there is a homomorphism, h, between two modules, $M, \bar{M}$ over the same ring and U is the subset of M that is mapped to zero by h, namely, the kernel of h, then the congruence classes $M|U$ is isomorphic to $\bar{M}$. Given the homomorphism theorem, Noether demonstrates that the two isomorphism theorems follow.

There are versions of both the homomorphism theorem and the isomorphism theorems in Dedekind's writings. But they are formulated in the context of groups and as arithmetical results. More importantly, they are not presented as being dependent on each other as in Noether's writings and certainly not in the general form that she gave them:

> [Dedekind] stated the isomorphism theorems as a way of counting cosets of his 'modules' – infinite additive subgroups of the complex numbers. Noether stated isomorphism theorems as dealing with isomorphisms and gave a uniform method of proving them from homomorphism theorems for many categories of structures – all groups, commutative groups, groups or commutative groups with a given domain of operators, all rings, commutative rings, rings with operators, and more. (McLarty 2006, p. 199)

---

[29] Herman Weyl (1995) attributes the style of thinking to Dirichlet, referring to the Dirichlet principle: 'to conquer problems with a minimum of blind computation with a maximum of insightful thoughts' (p. 453).

[30] Note further the similarities with the phenomenon 'reverse mathematics' as discussed in Section 1.2.1.

2.2.3 Bourbaki and Structures as a Tool

Various structural themes emerge in the work of Hilbert and Noether. Neither of them, though, says that mathematics is the study of structures. This changes in the writings of Bourbaki. Bourbaki explicitly claims that structures play a fundamental role in mathematics. In addition to giving a bit of background information, I shall focus on how Bourbaki characterises the axiomatic method and his conception of the fundamental structures of mathematics – the mother structures – and how they form the building blocks of modern mathematics.

Nicolas Bourbaki is the pseudonym of a group of mainly French mathematicians. One of their main accomplishments is the book series, *Éléments de Mathématique*, in English *Elements of Mathematics*. Another is their influence on how modern mathematics is conceived and done:

> The twentieth century has been, until recently, an era of 'modern mathematics' in the sense quite parallel to 'modern art' or 'modern architecture' or 'modern music'. That is to say, it turned to an analysis of abstraction, it glorified purity and tried to simplify its results until the roots of each idea were manifest. These trends started in the works of Hilbert in Germany, were greatly extended in France by the secret mathematical club known as 'Bourbaki', and found fertile soil in Texas, in the topological school of R. L. Moore. Eventually they conquered essentially the entire world of mathematics, even tried to breach the walls of high school in the disastrous episode of the 'new math'. (Mumford 1991)

The idea of the Bourbaki group was conceived in 1934 by André Weil and Henri Cartan who at the time were teaching at the university of Strasbourg. They were worried that French students were lagging behind after the war and found that one way to improve the situation would be to write an updated textbook in analysis. They presented the idea at one of their weekly Paris meetings with former student colleagues from l'École Normal and so the group was formed in 1935. Some of the first members included, besides Cartan and Weil, Claude Chevalley, Jean Delsarte, Jean Dieudonné and Charles Ehresman. Later other prominent mathematicians were invited to join, for example, Eilenberg, Grothendieck, Samuel and Serre. When formed, the group realised that they did not just need a book on analysis and so they decided to rewrite all of mathematics. A task that continues to this day.

The name 'Elements' refers to Euclid's *Elements*. Bourbaki's intention was to adapt the axiomatic style used in Hilbert's *Foundations of Geometry* and van der Waerden's *Moderne Algebra* and apply it more generally to all of mathematics.

Cartan (1980) notes that the axiomatic style as introduced by Hilbert and used by the German school of algebra (referring to Noether and her students) 'has penetrated the whole of mathematics' (Cartan, p. 176). Today Bourbaki's *Elements* comprise multiple volumes on topics such as algebra, topology, analysis, spectral theory and differential and analytic manifolds.

'The architecture of mathematics' (Bourbaki 1950) tells us how Bourbaki understands the axiomatic method. The method involves a few steps and is exemplified by the introduction of the structure of a group. In the first step one realises that seemingly differently looking collections have similar properties. Consider, for example, the collection of real numbers under addition, the collection of integers modulo a prime number p, and finally the displacements in 3-dimensional space under composition. Viewed as collections on which there is defined an operation, they are alike. In the next step, one investigates the logical structure of their shared properties and asks if a number of them suffice to derive the rest. In the given example, it is found that the axioms characterising a group have as a consequence the remaining shared properties.

As presented here, the method resembles to some degree Hilbert's description of how to deepen the foundations. But there are some noticeable differences. Bourbaki compares three different collections and *abstracts* from them to form the general concept of a group. The elements of the before-considered collections become empty positions. The only focus is on properties of the operations defined on them. Second, although Bourbaki mentions further foundational issues that are related to formal studies of mathematics, such as the consistency of the chosen axioms, he does not seem worried about these issues (see the introduction of Bourbaki (1960)). He does, however, share Hilbert's attitude regarding the fruitfulness of the axiomatic method. One advantage mentioned is that whenever we establish that a given collection fulfils the axioms of a group (or any of the other fundamental structures), we will know – at no further mental cost – that it also has all the properties of a group. As such the axiomatic method is associated with unification.[31] This is not the only mentioned advantage. He refers to the obtained structures as 'tools' giving examples of the advances made when realising that a given set or structure can be *represented in a different domain*. One such example is the geometric representation of the complex numbers which they write eventually enabled Gauss, Abel, Cauchy and Riemann to transform analysis. We return to Riemann's visual representation of complex functions in Section 3.

In regard to ontology, Cartan stresses that a structuralist view has the consequence that one gets rid of objects – mathematics concerns properties and

---

[31] The French title of their books, referring to 'mathématique' rather than 'mathématiques' is deliberately chosen to emphasise the unity of mathematics obtained by taking their approach. See Borel (1998, p. 374).

reasoning – and so mathematics is based on hypothetical reasoning: A mathematician having found a proof of a proposition will go through the proof to see which assumptions are actually required. 'Instead of declaring which objects are to be investigated, one has only to list the properties of the objects to be used in the investigation. These properties are then brought to the fore expressed by axioms; whereupon it ceases to be important to express what the objects *are*. Instead, the proof can be constructed in such a way as to hold true for every object that satisfies the axioms' (Cartan 1980, pp. 176–177).

A group is but one example of the algebraic structures. The algebraic structures constitute one of Bourbaki's fundamental structures referred to as 'mother structures'. These are the structures from which modern mathematics is built and constitute a sort of foundation for mathematics. Besides the algebraic structures, there are the order structures (i.e., collections on which there is defined an order relation) and the topological structures. These structures form the basic building blocks. In addition to these there are more specific structures and mixed structures that, together with the mother structures, constitute a hierarchy of structures. Specific structures are obtained by adding further properties, for example, considering abelian groups or finitely generated groups. We further encounter mixed structures: collections that have, or can be given, multiple structures. The set of real numbers is one example: 'the set of real numbers is provided with three kinds of structures: an algebraic structure, defined by arithmetical operations (addition and multiplication); an order structure, since inequalities are defined between real numbers; and finally a topological structure based on the notion of limit' (Cartan 1980, p. 177). Further examples abound and include topological groups, analytical fibre spaces and C^*-algebras.

The hierarchy of structures and the various interrelations between the different types of structure provide the means to organise all of mathematics. Bourbaki uses the metaphor 'the architecture of mathematics' for the picture of mathematics as founded on the mother structures. He likens mathematics with all its interrelations to a big city

> whose outlying districts and suburbs encroach incessantly, and in a somewhat chaotic manner, on the surrounding country, while the center is rebuilt from time to time, each time in accordance with a more clearly conceived plan and a more majestic order, tearing down the old sections with their labyrinths of alleys, and projecting towards the periphery new avenues, more direct, broader and more commodious. (Bourbaki 1950, p. 230)

2.2.4 Components of a Methodological Structuralism

We are now able to describe some of the components of a structuralist view of mathematics. One component consists of various facets of the axiomatic method. From one perspective, the axiomatic method can be seen as a tool to create structures. The individual axioms characterise relations between the considered entities, and together, a collection of axioms defines a structure such as a ring or a group. From another perspective, the method can be used to organise a theory, choosing which propositions should be taken as primitive, that is, as the foundation for the rest. Bourbaki refers to a different metaphor, that of a big city, for how mathematics is organised (and constantly re-organised); the axiomatic method is used to create the fundamental mother structures which are then combined and interrelate in multiple ways to form the complex that is mathematics. Note therefore that, although I refer to 'the' axiomatic method as used by Hilbert, Noether and Bourbaki, they do this in quite distinct ways with different outcomes and motivations.

A related theme is the shift of focus concerning the subject matter of mathematics; mathematics becomes the science of structures rather than individual objects. In some cases, it is even claimed that structuralism gets rid of objects and that there is no need to say anything about their nature; see Cartan's comment that mathematics is only based on reasoning and hypotheses that are formulated in the form of axioms. A structuralist view thus opens up for a hypothetical view of mathematics. I refer to Awodey (2004), Carter (2014) and Ferreirós (2016) for different positions that consider mathematics as hypothetical.

A second component concerns the different uses of 'structure'. In addition to the basic structures such as a group, topological space, and so on, we have noted the existence of structure theorems that say how entities of various sorts can be decomposed into simpler ones. Structure theorems come in various forms and constitute a useful tool in mathematics.[32] That is, mathematics does not only consider structures as 'units'. Structures may themselves have 'a structure' (which can be understood in different ways). Moreover there are relations, or interrelations between structures that we return to shortly.

The final component concerns the claim that the structural point of view (via the axiomatic method) is an effective tool in mathematics. Recall Hilbert's claim that the axiomatic method, namely, the deepening of foundations, considerations of independence, and so on, is a fruitful endeavour that has led to many new discoveries. Bourbaki further stresses the methodological point of view of structuralism. First is the role of unification, the identification of

---

[32] The type of decomposition depends on the objects and operations or relations defined on them. It consists of a product in the case of the Fundamental theorem of arithmetic, direct sums in algebra, exact sequences in algebraic topology, etc.

certain basic structures – the mother structures – that he uses to build mathematics. The second is the use of these basic structures to economise thought. The last subsection of this section considers in more detail the methodological aspect of structuralism. This aspect is further combined with the observation that mathematics rarely considers structures in isolation but exploits many different types of interrelations between them.[33]

2.3 The Role of Interrelations in Mathematics

Once it has been established that mathematics studies structures, one might ask how to characterise these structures and enquire about their nature and foundations. Questions like these are the focus of philosophical structuralism. Structuralism is often characterised by stating that objects only have so-called structural properties, that is, properties that depend on the relations that are defined on the structure in which they have a place. This follows, for example, from 'the view that mathematics is not concerned with the 'internal nature' of its objects, but rather how they relate to each other' (Korbmacher & Schiemer 2018, p. 295). Korbmacher and Schiemer observe, however, that texts rarely mention how structural properties are defined. A further point is that the properties of a structure depend on how one characterises a structure. Recall that a structure might be characterised axiomatically, stating that a collection of axioms characterises a given structure. In this case, properties of a given structure, a ring say, would consist of all the properties that can be derived from the axioms. It follows that all instantiations, or models, of a particular axiomatic description will have these properties. Another way to characterise the properties of a structure states that they are the properties that are shared by all systems instantiating a particular structure. Korbmacher and Schiemer demonstrate that these two definitions may lead to classes of properties that do not coincide.

If structuralism is supposed to capture what mathematics is about (broadly speaking), then the two mentioned characterisations of structure are too restrictive. Moreover, the way that properties are determined in mathematical practice is more varied. Properties depend to a large extent on different types of global relations, or interrelations between the considered structures. Moreover, mathematics formulates theorems about such interrelations. The remaining subsections of this section illustrate these claims.

---

[33] This point is also emphasised by Ferreirós and Reck (2020) in connection with Dedekind's work. They illustrate the claim by the example of Galois theory.

2.3.1 Formal Maps, Analogies and Representations

Relations between structures come in many shapes, ranging from formally specified maps to informal correspondences. They are exploited in various ways to determine properties of objects or structures. A formal map, for example, an isomorphism, between collections with different structure can be exploited to transfer properties from one collection to the other. Less formal correspondences may also be useful when looking for properties of a given structure. Consider as an example a finite field, $(F, +, \cdot)$. We might be interested to know something about its subfields. To do this, we notice that the field under multiplication (with the zero-object removed) has the structure of a group. We therefore consider the subset $F \setminus \{0\}$ of the field as a group under multiplication. Considered as a group, we may use Lagrange's theorem to tell us about its possible subgroups. (Lagrange's theorem states that the order of subgroups divides the order of the group). Equipped with the knowledge about possible subgroups, noting that they become possible subfields of F if one adds the zero-object, in combination with the fact that the order of finite fields are powers of primes, one may be able to say something about the subfields of F.

Another type of informal relation is analogy. Analogy is often mentioned as an important part of the mathematician's toolbox – in contemporary mathematics as well as historically:

> the most prolific and creative mathematicians like Archimedes, Johannes Kepler, John Wallis, Leibniz, Isaac Newton, Leonard Euler, Pierre Simon Laplace have underlined the eminent role of analogy in the discovery of new mathematical truths. This applies to mathematical concepts, methods, problems, proofs, rules, structures, symbolisms, theorems and theories. (Knobloch 2000, p. 296)

To this list one could add John von Neumann, who allegedly claimed that he considered his bicommutant theorem for von Neumann algebras as an analogue to the Galois correspondence, and Michael Atiyah stressing its importance in relation to the unification of mathematics (Atiyah 1978). More recent is Barry Mazur (2021) who writes that an analogy 'connects two disparate concepts by some similarity in their structure' (p. 12). Mazur considers as an example knots in 3-manifolds as analogous to primes of number fields which makes it possible to unify topological structures with arithmetic structures.[34] While highly useful, it is difficult to give a precise definition of an analogy. Characterisations range from stating that an analogy consists merely of 'perceived similarities' between domains to the actual identification of some 'shared structure'.

---

[34] Mazur further discusses the role of interconnections referred to as links, ties and bridges in contemporary mathematics.

The last interrelation to be considered here is representation. A representation is a sign that stands for some (mathematical) entity to somebody (who is the interpretant).[35] I consider cases where we represent a particular situation, sometimes referred to as the target, such as an expression, concept, relations between concepts, and so on. A representation, then, is often composed of other, more basic signs such as notational elements. When forming a representation, a specific correspondence, or rule, between the representation and the target is established. The correspondence is not always stated explicitly, but is exploited in practice. A simple example is when we consider the graph of a real function, $y = f(x)$, given by some expression. In this case, the convention is that corresponding values, x and $f(x)$, of the function are represented by the point $(x, f(x))$.

As an example of a fruitful representation, we consider C^*-algebras that can be represented by directed graphs. C^*-algebras generated by directed graphs are referred to as graph-algebras. A C^*-algebra can be characterised as a set (a vector space over the complex numbers) that has three types of structures (cf. Bourbaki's mixed structures). Each structure is given by a different type of operation: it has an algebraic structure obtained by the operations of addition and multiplication as well as multiplication by complex scalars. There is a norm defined on its elements which can be used to define a topology, and, finally, there is an involution operation, referred to as the *-operation. A C^*-algebra therefore has both an algebraic and a topological structure. The final operation, the *-operation, provides a link between the algebraic and topological structure.[36]

An important research question concerns the classification of C^*-algebras, that is, determining up to isomorphism which algebras are possible to define. A tool to achieve this is K-theory. The idea is that two C^*-algebras are isomorphic if their corresponding K-groups, K_0 and K_1, are pairwise isomorphic.[37] It turns out that it is generally quite complicated to calculate K-groups even for simple C^*-algebras. It has recently been discovered that a large class of C^*-algebras can be generated from directed graphs. One advantage of having this alternative form of representation is that it gives a much easier calculation of the K-groups. A directed graph is formally defined as a four-tuple: $\mathbf{D} = \{V, E, r, s\}$, where V consists of a collection of vertices v_i and E consists of edges e_i that each has a source and a range among the vertices. $r, s\colon E \to V$ are the range and source

---

[35] The definition is inspired by C. S. Peirce and adapted to a mathematical context. See also Section 3.3.3

[36] See the lecture notes by Ian Putnam (p. 8), www.math.uvic.ca/faculty/putnam/ln/C*-algebras.pdf.

[37] This is not true in general, but K-theory is nevertheless considered as an important tool in the field.

Figure 2 A visual representation of a directed graph
with four vertices and five edges.

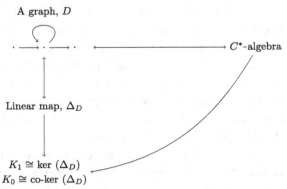

Figure 3 A directed graph generates a C^*-algebra and gives rise to a linear
map from which the two K-groups can be calculated.

maps that inform about the range and source of all the edges. Figure 2 shows
an example of a directed graph.

A particular graph can be read according to a specified rule to define generators and relations between them which together generate a specific C^*-algebra.
Read in a different way, one obtains a linear map from which it is possible to
calculate the two K-groups, K_1 and K_0 (as the kernel and co-kernel of the linear
map, respectively). See Raeburn and Szymanski (2004) and Carter (2018) for
details. Figure 3 illustrates the connections.

One point in this example is that mathematics frequently represents problems
in other domains where they become easier (or even possible) to solve. Another
point concerns the fact that for such representations to be useful, one needs
first to establish formal relations between the domains. In the case considered,
there are theorems that establish the connections, for example, a theorem that
mentions the correspondences shown in Figure 3 – roughly:

*If D is a directed graph subject to some conditions and Δ_D a particular map,
then the co-kernel of Δ_D is isomorphic to K_0 of the graph algebra generated
from D and the kernel of Δ_D is isomorphic to K_1 of the graph algebra generated
from D.* (Raeburn and Szymanski 2004, theorem 3.2)

Mathematics is also *about* these connections – not only the individual structures
such as a C^*-algebra. Furthermore, we determine properties of C^*-algebras by

exploiting this connection (and others like it). I illustrate these claims in more detail with a simpler example on the complex numbers.

2.3.2 Representations of Complex Numbers

Besides serving as an illustration of the usefulness of represention in mathematics and how this depends on established correspondences, the complex numbers have given rise to a much discussed problem. The challenge is that a certain structuralist position, the so-called non-eliminative structuralism, seems to entail that we are not able to distinguish between the two complex numbers i and $-i$ (Keränen 2001). Non-eliminative structuralism holds that structures are in the ontology (they cannot be 'eliminated') and mathematical objects are considered as places in structures. Furthermore, places have only structural properties. The problem of indiscernibles occurs when one asks about the identity conditions of places. Considering the complex numbers as an algebraic field, Keränen argues that there is no relation that makes it possible to distinguish between i and $-i$. An obvious candidate is an automorphism, but conjugation (which is an automorphism on $\mathbb{C}$) takes i to $-i$ and vice versa. There is a mathematical solution to this problem. McLarty (2020) notes that our ability to distinguish between the two complex numbers depends on whether we consider the complex numbers as an algebraic structure or as part of complex analysis. In the context of algebra, complex conjugation is an automorphism, whereas in complex analysis, it is not.

There are a number of ways to introduce the complex numbers. A textbook in complex analysis defines them as ordered pairs of real numbers, $\mathbb{C} = \{(x,y)|x,y \in \mathbb{R}\}$, equipped with addition and multiplication:

$$(x,y) + (a,b) = (x + a, y + b), \quad (x,y) \cdot (a,b) = (xa - yb, xb + ya)$$

$(\mathbb{C}, +, \cdot)$ so defined can be shown to be a field. i is defined as the element $(0,1)$. (It follows that $-i$ is the number $-(0,1) = (0,-1)$).

After introducing different representations of the numbers the authors comment:

> We now have five different ways of thinking about a complex number: the formal definition, in rectangular form, in polar form, and geometrically, using Cartesian coordinates or polar coordinates. *Each of these five ways is useful in different situations, and translating between them is an essential ingredient in complex analysis.* (Beck et al. 2002–18, p. 9 my emphasis)

It is possible to perform basic calculations such as addition and multiplication on numbers from the given definition. But when it comes to other types of calculations, some of the other ways of treating the complex numbers are more

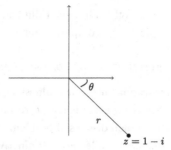

Figure 4 The complex number $z = 1 - i$ represented in a Cartesian coordinate system that also shows the polar coordinates (r, θ).

convenient. Let us consider an example. Suppose we wish to calculate the 6th power of the number $z = 1 - i$ (now presented in the rectangular form). In order to do this we represent the number in polar form. We first consider the corresponding coordinates $(1, -1)$ in a Cartesian coordinate system and notice that the point can also be characterised by the length, r, of the line segment between the point and the origin (referred to as the modulus) and the angle, θ, that this line makes with the positive x-axis (the argument). That is, it can be determined by the polar coordinates (r, θ); see Figure 4. The corresponding polar form of representation is $z = r(\cos \theta + i \cdot \sin \theta) = r \cdot e^{\theta \cdot i}$.

The first task is to determine the values of r and θ, that is, establish a correspondence between the two forms of representation. Noticing that we have a right angled triangle, we can use a trigonometric relation, for example, $\tan(\theta) = y/x$, and Pythagoras' theorem to determine the two numbers. We write z in the polar form as $z = \sqrt{2}(\cos(-\pi/4) + i \cdot \sin(-\pi/4)) = \sqrt{2} \cdot e^{-(\pi/4) \cdot i}$.

Before we can perform the calculation, we need to establish what the operations defined on the Cartesian coordinates correspond to in the new form of representation. Using a variety of trigonometric identities, it is possible to show that multiplication of two numbers given in polar coordinates, (r_1, θ_1) and (r_2, θ_2), is given by $(r_1 \cdot r_2, \theta_1 + \theta_2)$. That is, the modulus of the product is the product of the moduli of the multiplied terms and the argument is found by adding the given arguments. Using this fact, it is easy to calculate the result:

$$z^6 = (\sqrt{2} \cdot e^{-(\pi/4) \cdot i})^6 = (\sqrt{2})^6 \cdot e^{6 \cdot (-(\pi/4) \cdot i)} = 8 \cdot e^{-(3\pi/2) \cdot i}$$

The geometric representation of the complex numbers is not only a useful tool when performing simple calculations on them. The geometric representation of complex numbers turned out to be extremely fruitful in the hands of Riemann as previously mentioned. Riemann (1851) represented complex functions visually and was thereby able to formulate their characterising property in geometric terms, see Section 3.3.2. Riemann further considered the multivalued Abelian functions and found a way to represent them by Riemann surfaces. This example illustrates well that a representation in a different context sometimes paves the way to a whole new field, a field that does not seem imaginable from the original form of presentation. In the next section, we consider this example as well as other examples of fruitful representations and discuss some of their properties.

3 Visual Thinking in Mathematics

Throughout history, visual representations, or diagrams, have played a significant role in mathematics. This is particularly true of the mathematics of the ancient Greeks as documented by Netz (1999). Around the turn of the twentieth century, however, one finds statements by mathematicians, such as Pasch and Hilbert, and philosophers saying that diagrams should be excluded in mathematical proofs. Pasch puts it in the following way:

> For the appeal to a figure is, in general, not at all necessary. It does facilitate essentially the grasp of the relations stated in the theorem and the constructions applied in the proof. Moreover, it is a fruitful tool to discover such relationships and constructions. However, if one is not afraid of the sacrifice of time and effort involved, then one can omit the figure in the proof of any theorem; indeed, the theorem is only truly demonstrated if the proof is completely independent of the figure. (Pasch 1882/1926, 43) (Quote and translation from Mancosu 2005, p. 14)

Russell (1901) agrees, writing that 'in the best books there are no figures at all' (Russell 1901, p. 99). We noted in the first section that Russell sought to provide mathematics with a logical foundation. He explains that when inferences are based on figures, we may be misled. Only when figures are omitted and reasoning is put in a strict symbolic form is it possible to detect which assumptions are required. This view of diagrams appears to have been adopted by mathematicians in general sometime after 1900: The number of diagrams in published articles drops visibly in the period between 1910 and 1950 (Johansen & Pallivicini 2022).[38] Today diagrams abound in mathematical practice; they are drawn and referred to in informal discussions among mathematicians, in colloquia, and found in textbooks as well as in articles. Natural questions, then, arise regarding the roles these diagrams play and whether they can have an essential role in proofs.

---

[38] Johansen and Pallavicini blame the 'formalist view' of mathematics for the reduced number of diagrams in the journals. There could be other reasons as well; for example, a change of topics that are studied in the considered period.

We consider two aspects of these questions. One is the use of diagrams in mathematical proofs, from their use in Euclid's *Elements* to more recent mathematics and logic. This is the topic of the first two subsections. The second concerns the heuristic role of visual representations in mathematics, in particular how they lead to new discoveries. For this purpose, Section 3.3 examines the practice of constructing, manipulating and observing visual representations. In general, the section illustrates how some questions or problems can be approached by an examination and detailed analysis of exemplary case studies. I refer to Giaquinto (2007 and 2020) on the epistemic use of visual representations in mathematical practice more generally. In *Visual Thinking in Mathematics* (2007), Marcus Giaquinto extensively discusses how visual representations contribute to mathematical knowledge, exploring their roles in both proofs and discoveries.

Before looking into the role of diagrams in contemporary mathematical practice, I provide a brief historical account of their use, starting with their significance in Greek mathematics, and mention some of the events that led to their rejection during the latter part of the nineteenth century.

3.1 Diagrams in Euclid's *Elements*

It is well known that diagrams formed an essential component of propositions as well as demonstrations in Greek mathematics. Reviel Netz (1999) analyses their role revealing a mutual dependence between text and diagrams. From this, he infers that diagrams serve as metonyms for their propositions. The interdependence between diagram and text is supported by a number of observations. In some cases the diagram has to be consulted to locate a particular point, since it is not fully specified in the accompanying text (Netz refers to these points as 'completely unspecified'). Suppose, for example, that I tell you that AB is the radius of a circle and that the line segment BC is twice the length of AB. In this case, the point C is completely unspecified. (A and B are underspecified since we are not able to tell which point is the centre and which lies on the circumference of the circle – but we do know something about their location.) Netz has found that about 19 per cent of points in the *Elements* book XIII are completely unspecified (section 2.1, p. 23). An important role of the accompanying diagram, then, is to fix the reference of such points. Moreover, information that is used in demonstrations, is read off from diagrams. Conversely, the text tells you how to read the diagram. Another observation is based on an analysis of the ancient Greeks' use of the word 'diagram' that seems to refer to the proposition itself and not the accompanying figure. Finally, Netz notes that each proposition has a unique diagram so that the diagram individuates its proposition: You see the diagram and you can tell at an instant which proposition is at stake.

Whereas Netz informs us about the role of diagrams in Greek mathematics in general, Ken Manders (2008a,b) focuses on the validity of the diagram-based tradition in Euclidean plane geometry. He comments on the paradoxical circumstance that the plane geometry of Euclid's *Elements* has served as an inspiration for many mathematicians and even formed the foundation for mathematics for over two thousand years after it was written, while contemporary scholars seem to reject its methods:

> It was a stable and fruitful tool of investigation across diverse cultural contexts for over two thousand years. During that time, it generally struck thoughtful and knowledgeable people as the most rigorous of human ways of knowing, even in the face of centuries of internal criticism in antiquity. (Manders 2008b, p. 80)

The classic paper 'The Euclidean Diagram' (Manders 2008b, written in 1995) rationally reconstructs the underlying practice of the ancient Greeks explaining its epistemic success. I shall give an outline of some of the components of this practice.

The first component concerns the inferences of the *Elements*. An inference in Euclidean plane geometry takes as input either a piece of information taken from the text or an attribute read off from the accompanying diagram, or both. The conclusion is either a new piece of textual information or a new diagram element. Figure 5 illustrates the general structure of an inference. To see how it is used we consider proposition I.1 which tells us how to construct an equilateral triangle on a given finite straight line. The given straight line is AB. In the construction part of the demonstration one is asked to draw a circle with centre A and radius AB. That is, based on textual input 'AB is a line segment' and postulate 3, granting the construction of the circle, the output of the inference consists of a new diagram element, a circle. A second circle is drawn with B as centre and AB as radius. It is noticed that they intersect in a point, C. By drawing lines between A and C, and then between B and C, one obtains a triangle; see Figure 6. In the remaining part of the demonstration, it is proved that the constructed triangle is equilateral, that is, the sides are equal. A step in this proof is to notice that AB and AC are both radii of the same circle and are

claims in prior text	and/or	*attributions to current diagram*
new claims in text	or	*new elements in diagram*

Figure 5 An illustration of inferences of the *Elements* as shown in Manders (2008a, p. 69)

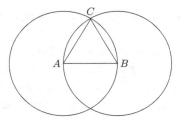

Figure 6 The diagram of Euclid I.1: To construct an equilateral triangle on a given line segment.

therefore equal. That is, this argument takes as input an attribute observed in the diagram and textual information, that radii of a circle are equal (definition 15), to conclude that the two line segments are equal.

Since an inference may depend on attributes from the accompanying diagram, it is relevant to consider which *type* of information is read off. For this purpose, Manders has introduced the notions of co-exact and exact attributes. A co-exact attribute is a property that is not changed by continuous variations of the diagram (Manders 2008b, p. 92). Examples of co-exact attributes are the crossing of the circles in proposition I.1, that a region or line segment is contained in another, and so on. An exact attribute is, for example, that two line segments or angles are equal. Manders has analysed all cases where information is read off from a diagram in Euclid's plane geometry. It turns out that they are all instances of co-exact properties. In addition, a number of formal systems that model Euclid's geometry have been formulated with the intent to show that it is valid. Jeremy Avigad and John Mumma (2009) present one such formal system that is based on Manders' reconstruction.

A consequence of the observation that information is sometimes read off from diagrams is that a particular diagram must make a clear case for the attributes it is supposed to display. Manders places such considerations under the heading of 'diagram discipline'. To be able to reliably read off information from a particular diagram requires that it must have a suitable size (not too small or too big) and that it is kept sufficiently simple. The latter is accomplished by, for example, splitting propositions into many parts: It takes 47 propositions to reach to the main theorem of book I, Pythagoras' theorem. In addition, what the diagram displays seems to be carefully chosen (see also Catton and Montelle (2012)). On the other hand, the reasoning practice also places demands on the agents, trusting that they read off diagram attributes uniformly. This is made possible by keeping the number of responses small; only around 30 types of responses are required. Agents are supposed to be able to recognise the various (simple) geometrical figures such as triangles, the crossing of lines, and containment relations.[39]

The final component considers the agents that constitute the practice and their roles in forming an epistemically valid practice. In addition to the role of agents making a case that a given proposition holds is the role of the opponent. This is referred to as 'probing' and can take two different forms. One type of criticism consists of an objection that a proposed diagram does not make a clear enough case for the co-exact attributes that agents are supposed to read off. That is, the opponent criticises the diagram's appearance. Objections of this sort may also prevent the fallacious diagram that leads to the conclusion that all triangles are isosceles. The second type of probing questions the generality of the drawn diagram and might result in case branching.

Both the structure and the geometric content of the *Elements* have inspired mathematicians long after it was written. The structure, that is, building mathematics on definitions and axioms has served as an ideal for how to present theoretical sciences. Furthermore, geometry has for long served as a foundation in many areas of mathematics. This is in particular the case in the early history of analysis, studying the properties of curves.[40] When determining the tangent (or sub-tangent) to a curve, properties of similar triangles are quite useful. Take Pierre de Fermat as an example. He considers (in 1638) the curve *CA*, see Figure 7, and a tangent placed at point *A*. The sub-tangent of the curve at point *A* corresponds to the line segment *BD* along (what we would refer to as) the *x*-axis. In order to determine this line segment, Fermat considers another point, *E* (which is located on the tangent, not the curve). We then see that two similar triangles appear, that is, triangle *DFE* and *DBA*. Fermat exploits the fact that the sides of these triangles have similar proportions and utilises the expression of the curve in question to determine the given line segment.[41]

A few years later Isaac Newton used the same geometric relation (referring to a figure that is similar to the one shown in Figure 7) to determine the value

---

[39] The latter is seen in, for example, proposition II.11 where a particular rectangle is observed to be part of two different rectangles.

[40] Geometry also played an important part in the early history of algebra, namely in equation solving. The Arabic mathematicians from around 800 (e.g., Al Khwarizmi) formulated algorithms to solve quadratic equations, but based their demonstrations on geometry. Much later, in Cardano's *Ars Magna* published in 1545, there are still geometric traces. The solution of cubic equations is given in terms of a line segment, and cubic identities are obtained by considering partitions of a cube.

[41] Fermat also uses geometric arguments and the results of geometric series to calculate quadratures; he was even able to formulate a version of partial integration using intricate geometric arguments. The results are written around 1659 in a treatise on methods of quadrature.

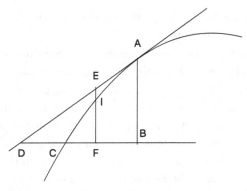

Figure 7 Fermat determines the sub-tangent of a curve in 1638.

of the sub-tangent as $T = \frac{\dot{x}}{\dot{y}} \cdot y$. Newton's framework is, of course, fundamentally different, as by then he had developed his version of the differential and integral calculus with new terminology and theoretical background. Therefore, Newton's sub-tangent is obtained by an application of one of his fundamental propositions of calculus that tells us how to calculate the relation between the two fluxions, $\dot{x}$ and $\dot{y}$, given a relation between the fluents.

After Newton's and Leibniz's inventions of calculus in the second part of the 17th century, figures gradually disappear from calculus texts. Leonard Euler's book on differential calculus (published in 1755) contains no figures. Euler explicitly comments on this fact in the preface: 'everything is kept within the bounds of pure analysis, so that in the explanation of the rules of this calculus there is no need for any geometric figures' (Euler 1755/2000, p. xii). Euler introduces the concept of a function, defined as an analytic expression, and further develops his differential calculus based on the methods and notation introduced by Leibniz. Thereby calculus can be considered as rules on how to operate on analytic expressions rather than working with geometric properties of curves. More surprisingly, perhaps, is that Cauchy's textbooks for teaching analysis at the École Polytechnique[42] in the early nineteenth century do not contain a single figure either.

During the nineteenth century one finds explicit statements that geometric intuition cannot be relied on in analysis and multiple examples are given showing why this is the case. An often mentioned example is the possibility of formulating the expression of a continuous function that is nowhere differentiable (proved by Weierstrass in 1861). This example, as well as Peano's

---

[42] They are Cours d'Analyse (1821) and Resumé des leçons données a l'École Polytechnique sur le calcul infinitesimal (1823).

space-filling curve were later mentioned by Hans Hahn (1933/1980) as reasons why geometric intuition cannot be relied on in the article 'The crisis of intuition'. There is a similar development in geometry as is evident from the quotes of Pasch and Hilbert. But the reasons why figures disappear from mathematics texts in general after the eighteenth century have not, to my knowledge, been completely explained.

3.2 Diagrams in Contemporary Mathematics and Logic

During the 1990s – the same time as Manders was defending diagram-based reasoning in the *Elements* – philosophers and mathematicians were making a case that it is possible to formulate rigorous proofs based on diagrams, pointing to the fact that contemporary mathematicians sometimes seem to rely on figures or diagrams. The logicians Barwise and Etchemendy (1996) have constructed what is referred to as heterogenous logical systems and thereby argue that proofs can contain diagrammatic elements. To illustrate this point we show later an example of a formal diagram system – the alpha part of Peirce's Existential Graphs – as described in (Shin 2002). Besides demonstrating that it is possible to formulate sound diagrammatic systems of logic, the aim is to convey some of the other interesting properties that such systems might have.

Vaughan Jones (1998) is among the mathematicians who object to the view that proofs can only be acceptable in case they are presented in a formal, symbolic language. Criticising more broadly the view that a formal proof is all there is to truth in mathematics, he writes:

> Proofs are indispensable, but I would say they are necessary but not sufficient for mathematical truth, at least truth as perceived by the individual. (Jones 1998, p. 208)

Jones provides a number of examples in support of this view, including a result from knot theory, Alexander's closed braid theorem. He offers a picture proof of this theorem, a proof that is based on manipulations on knot diagrams, commenting that it would be hopeless to review in case it was presented as a formal proof.

More recently Silvia De Toffoli and Valeria Giardino (2014) have made a case that diagrams play an epistemic role in contemporary low-dimensional topology. They claim that mathematicians conceive of diagrams as 'dynamic inferential tools that are modified and produced for epistemic purposes' (p. 830). Their examples range from considering different presentations of knots to a picture proof in a topology textbook that two presentations of the Poincaré homology sphere are equivalent. The proof presented in the textbook

Knots and links[43] simply consists of a series of figures and specified rules indicate how to mentally manipulate them.

Besides discussing whether reasoning based on diagrams is rigorous, one may consider the advantages that diagrammatic systems have over symbolic systems. We illustrate some of these advantages by C. S. Peirce's graphic logic, his Existential Graphs (EGs), as reconstructed in Shin (2002). Peirce constructed three different versions of EGs, the alpha, beta and gamma systems corresponding to propositional, first-order and modal logic respectively. Sun-Joo Shin insists that Peirce's EGs should be assessed on their own terms, that is, one should consider the features made possible because of their iconic nature. 'Iconic' refers to Peirce's semiotics. An icon is a sign that represents because of some shared likeness with the object it stands for (see Section 3.3.3 for further details). She also notes that the alpha and beta versions of the EGs correspond, respectively, to propositional and first-order classical logic, which entails that they are both sound and complete.

We consider two properties of the EGs. One is the iconic reading of the graphs. Another advantage is that they can be systematically read in different ways, providing easy access to logical equivalent expressions. We illustrate these claims in the case of the alpha part of the EGs. The basic building blocks of this system are statement variables (or just the statements themselves) and two logical operations corresponding to conjunction and negation. There is no visible sign corresponding to 'and': the rule is that whenever two propositions are written on what Peirce refers to as the sheet of assertion, one intends their conjunction. That is, if I see a tree with white flowers and that the sky is blue, I can write this on the sheet of assertion:

The sky is blue   The tree has white flowers

Shin argues that Peirce's decision not to have a physical sign that denotes 'and' turns it into an iconic representation of the conjunction of two facts. To see why, note that what I have written corresponds exactly to what I observe. I see that the sky is blue, I see the tree – but there is nothing in what I see that corresponds to the 'and' or the '∧' that we use in the linear form of propositional logic.[44]

---

[43] See p. 325 of Rolfsen, D. [1976]. Knots and links. Publish or Perish, Inc., Berkeley.

[44] Peirce explains this choice in a paper 'On existential graphs, Euler's diagrams, and logical algebra' from ca. 1903, see (CP 4.418–4.507). CP 4.418 refers to Peirce's Collected Papers (Peirce 1965–67) book 4 and paragraph 418. He writes the following about conjunction: 'A diagram ought to be as iconic as possible; that is, it should represent relations by visible relations analogous to them. ... Each proposition is true independently of the other, and either may therefore be expressed on the sheet of assertion. If both are written on different parts of the sheet of

If we write B for the statement 'the sky is blue' and W for 'the tree has white flowers', the conjunctive proposition can be written as

$$W$$

$$B$$

Note that the location of these statements on the sheet does not affect the logical status of the proposition. The preceding graph can thus be read both as 'B and W' and 'W and B'.

A negation in this system is referred to as a 'cut' and is marked by a closed curve enclosing the negated proposition as shown in Figure 8. The interpretation of this graph is 'it is not the case that W' or 'the tree does not have white flowers'. Note again that an iconic interpretation of the sign, the cut, is possible. This time metaphorically, taking the name of the rule into account, and understanding negation as 'cutting out' a particular statement that is not true. (Imagine that you are writing statements on a piece of paper and discover that one is not true. You draw a closed line around it to indicate that it should be ripped out.)

A number of different graphs are shown in Figure 9. According to Peirce's intended reading, the 'endoporeutic' reading, they correspond to the following propositions.

(i)   P and Q
(ii) not P
(iii) not (P and not Q)
(iv) not (not P and not Q)

Shin explains how it is possible to introduce different reading strategies on these graphs. One is to read graph (iii) in Figure 9 as $P \rightarrow Q$.[45] (Exploiting

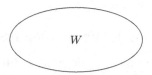

Figure 8 An existential graph representing 'not W'.

---

assertion, the independent presence on the sheet of the two expressions is analogous to the independent truth of the two propositions that they would, when written separately assert' (CP 4.433).

[45] Peirce explains the iconicity of this reading in the previously mentioned paper 'On existential graphs, Euler's diagrams, and logical algebra' (see the previous footnote). He first notices that

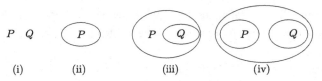

$$P \quad Q$$

(i)   (ii)   (iii)   (iv)

Figure 9 Examples of existential graphs.

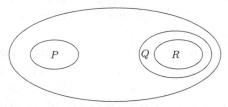

Figure 10 An existential graph with multiple readings. Reading the graph as having the form of a disjunct, one may obtain $P \vee (Q \wedge \neg R)$. Read using implication from the right we see, for example, $(Q \rightarrow R) \rightarrow P$.

that this is equivalent to $\neg(P \wedge \neg Q$.) Another reading strategy reads graph (iv) as $P \vee Q$.

Consider next the graph in Figure 10. Using the given reading strategies, the graph can be read in a number of ways. Using cut and 'and', reading from the outside and in (i.e., Peirce's original reading method) the graph is read as $\neg(\neg P \wedge \neg(Q \wedge \neg R))$. If we instead notice that it has the 'form' of the operation 'or', we may read it as $P \vee (Q \wedge \neg R)$. On a third reading, we observe that the outer cut encloses two cuts of different orders and read it using implication from the left: $\neg P \rightarrow (Q \wedge \neg R)$, or implication from the right to obtain $\neg(Q \wedge \neg R) \rightarrow P$. Since all of these are read from the same graph, they are all equivalent. These advantages suggest that diagrams can be fruitful tools in mathematics. This is indeed the case. The next section explores further this aspect of visual representations.

3.3 Diagrams as Effective Representations

In addition to the iconic features of diagrams and the epistemic advantages obtained by controlled multiple readings, visual representations also give rise to new concepts, relations and proofs (see, for example, Carter (2010)) or even

---

implication is analogous to the geometrical relation of inclusion (CP 4.435). He therefore finds that it is reasonable 'that one of the two compartments should be placed within the other' and concludes that it must be the consequent that is placed in the inner compartment (introducing the scroll).

fields as in the case of Riemann's contributions (see also Starikova (2010)). In the following we address the question of whether it is possible to explain how visual representations lead to new insights in mathematics. Section 3.3.2 analyses how the notion of a 'free ride' Shimojima (2001) applies to mathematics. Roughly, a free ride is a consequential piece of information that can be read off from a diagram, but has not deliberately been added when constructing it. Finally, in Section 3.3.3 we consider visual representations as an instance of iconic representations that can be manipulated, or experimented on.

3.3.1 What Is a Diagram?

When discussing the role of diagrams it is often useful to contrast them with other types of representation such as sentential representations. Similarly, when investigating the properties of fruitful representations it may beneficial to determine whether they rely on characterising properties specific to diagrams or if they hold more generally. It is therefore appropriate to state what a 'diagram' is. When referring to visual representations, it is common to distinguish between external and internal representations. Internal representations refer to mental images produced by our visual imagery whereas external representations are signs that are written or constructed on some physical media such as a piece of paper or a blackboard. In the following we consider only external representations.

Many different types of representations are used in mathematics; among visual representations there are diagrams, figures, graphs, tables and illustrations. See, for example, Bertin (2011) for a distinction between some of these. Another category consists of sentential representations, where it may be relevant to distinguish between natural language and mathematical expressions (that are formed using mathematical notation). It may not even be clear to which category mathematical expressions belong.

There are further cases where a characterisation of 'diagram' is useful. We mentioned the question whether proofs can be based on diagrams. Responses to this question depend on what type of information can reliably be read off from diagrams and diagram discipline (Manders 2008b) or whether diagrams can be considered to be a type of formal system (Shin 2002). One might also argue that diagrams (or a subclass of them) constitute a notation (Goodman 1976, pp. 170–171) and that they therefore can be parts of proofs. I refer to the forthcoming Element by Dirk Schlimm for a philosophy of notations.

In the philosophy of mathematics only a few contributions explicitly say what diagrams are, but in information and visualisation theory there are a number of proposals on how to characterise diagrams in contrast to other types of

$$E \qquad\qquad\qquad F$$

Figure 11 Two directed graphs, E and F.

representations such as natural languages.[46] Keith Stenning (2000) and Atsushi Shimojima (2001) discuss a number of proposed distinctions between diagrams and sentential representations in the context of information theory. Their aims, however, differ. Whereas Stenning seeks to understand how diagrams communicate, Shimojima notices that graphic representations hold the capacity to offer 'free rides' and wishes to explain this feature. Some of their distinctions make sense also in the context of mathematics. An often mentioned difference between diagrams and sentential representations is the apparent two-dimensionality of diagrams in contrast to the linearity of sentential representations. Several counter examples have been offered, however, arguing that this distinction is neither sufficient nor necessary. One is the use of two-dimensional notations, for example exponentials, in mathematics. Another type of counter-example consists of linear representations that intuitively seem to be diagrams such as the linear graph, E, shown in Figure 11. Whereas this distinction concerns the appearance of the representations, it is also possible to make a distinction based on how they are interpreted, that is, their semantics. Stenning (2000) notes that sentential representations are read and interpreted in a fixed direction, often from left to right, reading one character at a time, as when reading this text. In contrast, diagrams need not be interpreted in a fixed direction. Because of this, it is possible to read a particular diagram in multiple ways (as we noticed about Peirce's existential graphs and graph-algebras in Section 2.3.1). It is therefore of vital importance to supply rules that say how a particular diagram should be read.

Another distinction that sometimes applies considers whether letters, points and other basic components act as types or as tokens. In sentential representations, letters typically are taken as types. The 't' in 'typically' and in 'type' both refer to the same letter, the type 't', regardless of its location on this page.

---

[46] A recent discussion of how to characterise 'diagram' in a mathematical context is De Toffoli (2022). De Toffoli's main focus is to analyse the role of notations in mathematics and the possibility of considering mathematical diagrams as part of a notation.

In diagrams, it is often the case that the reference of a character or sign is determined by its location, that is, the same letter, say, placed at two different locations means that they refer to two different objects. Consider the graphs in Figure 11. They are composed of points and arrows placed at different locations. It is implicitly understood that the different points (and arrows) do not refer to the same, but to different vertices (or edges). The type of reference in this case is denoted token-reference whereas the first is type-reference.

A final distinction concerns how reasoning is displayed or the representation is formed. When making calculations in sentential representations one usually rewrites the transformed expression below or next to the previous one when making changes. This is referred to as discursive reasoning. When operating on diagrams, it is possible to add information successively to the same representation, as we shall see, forming agglomerative representations.

I offer the following characterisation of diagrams that I find useful when discussing the heuristic role of diagrams, in particular the question why they sometimes contribute new insights (see also Carter (2021, 2018)). It is not intended as a sharp distinction between different types of representations which I doubt is possible. First, I consider and distinguish between three different levels: the visual appearance of the representation, its semantics and, finally, how it is used. When considering the appearance of a representation, I note that mathematical representations are typically composed of certain basic elements according to syntactic rules. The basic constituents of diagrams consist of geometric elements such as points, line segments and curves and other types of notational elements such as letters (standing for mathematical objects). The syntactic rules of diagrams further allow production of two-dimensional objects. The syntactic rules of directed graphs, for example, make it possible to form two-dimensional displays as shown by the graph, F, in Figure 11. Similarly, some of the basic constituents of the *Elements* are line segments that can be composed into complex two-dimensional figures. The exponential expression referred to earlier may be considered as a notational unit. The syntax, however, makes it possible to compose exponentials into two-dimensional displays. The reason that they are not diagrams, I propose, is because of their semantics. Sentential representations come with a fixed reading direction (which is the case for exponentials; we must not confuse 2^3 with 3^2) whereas diagrams typically may be read in multiple directions according to specified rules. Finally, the uses of a particular representation may draw on the beforementioned distinctions between type and token reference and agglomerative versus discursive reasoning, where token reference and agglomerative reasoning are effective ways of using diagrammatic representations.

3.3.2 Free Rides in Mathematics

Suppose you are given the following information about three sets, A, B and C, that A and B are disjoint and that C is a subset of B. Formally, $A \cap B = \emptyset$ and $C \subseteq B$. The phenomenon of a free ride can be illustrated by representing these two facts by so-called Euler diagrams. Euler diagrams are constructed by using the convention that a set is represented by a closed curve in the plane such as a circle, and that elements of the set are contained inside the closed domain. It follows that a circle that is fully contained in another represents set inclusion and that two non-intersecting circles represent disjoint sets. According to this convention the given information leads to the configuration shown in Figure 12.

Observing the diagram, one notices that the two circles marked C and A do not overlap. This translates into the set theoretic claim that $A \cap C = \emptyset$. Since this is a piece of information that was not put into the representation when we constructed it, it is consequential information that comes for free, that is, what Shimojima calls a free ride. Notice also that Proposition I.1 in the *Elements* contains a free ride: The consequential piece of information that is possible to read off is the point of intersection between the two drawn circles.

The property that we read off from the Euler diagram follows from topological properties of the plane. The diagram consists of two non-intersecting circles, marked A and B and another circle that is fully contained in circle B. It is then impossible for circle C to have any points in common with circle A. That is, the free ride depends on geometric or topological properties of the representation itself. Shimojima denotes geometric, topological (and physical) properties of a representation as *nomic constraints* of the representation and argues that they govern free rides. It is not important for our concerns exactly what this involves; I refer to (Shimojima 2001) for details. We focus instead on free rides as they occur in mathematical practice and extend the notion accordingly.

My recent article ' "Free rides" in mathematics' (Carter 2021) analyses a number of occurrences of mathematical free rides. Some of the examples resemble the ones considered earlier: free rides depend on geometric and topological properties of the representations. But this is not always the case. Free rides, defined as 'consequential pieces of information that can be read

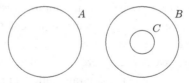

Figure 12 A diagrammatic representation of $A \cap B = \emptyset$ and $C \subseteq B$.

off from a diagram,' occurring in mathematics are more varied. In some cases they depend on the fact that diagrams allow multiple readings and theoretical results that connect these readings. This is the case in the example of graph-algebras that we presented in Section 2.3.1. A graph-algebra is a certain type of C^*-algebra that can be represented by directed graphs. An advantage is that the directed graphs can be read in two distinct ways. One reading of these graphs gives generators and relations that define a C^*-algebra, referred to as a graph-algebra. When read in a different way, one obtains a linear map from which it is easy to calculate the two K-groups of the C^*-algebra. Formal results establish the connection between the linear map and the corresponding C^*-algebra (Raeburn & Szymanski 2004).

In other cases the essential feature is a combination of the possibility to form two-dimensional displays with what was referred to as agglomerative reasoning. One of the considered examples is a commutative diagram from category theory that is read as a map in order to see that different expressions are identical. That the considered morphisms are successively added to the same diagram is as essential to the use of it as is its two-dimensionality. We illustrate these features by looking at Riemann's geometric representation of the property that characterises a complex function. We return to this example in the next section. Further details can be found in Carter (2021, pp. 10484–10486).

Riemann (1851) defines a function of a complex variable, $z = x + i \cdot y$, stating that $f(z) = u + i \cdot v$ is a complex function if the differential quotient $\frac{df}{dz}$ is independent of dz. (Today we would say that a function so defined is differentiable at z.) He further comments that this idea is easier to grasp when using one's 'spatial intuition' and so represents values of the variable and the function in different planes as illustrated in Figure 13. Using this geometric representation, he was able to express geometrically the condition of being a complex function. The condition entails that the two angles v and w will be identical and that the two triangles shown are similar. That is, the free ride that is obtained in this case is the similarity of the triangles. Note that we do not observe this fact. It is calculated based on visual information that it is possible to represent the difference between points (e.g., $dz = z - z_1$) in polar coordinates. (See Section 2.3.3 on different forms of presentations of complex numbers.) Inserting differences expressed in polar coordinates in the expression $\frac{df}{dz} = \frac{df}{dz'}$, it is possible to derive the result.

Returning to the preceding points, note that it is crucial that the objects considered are added to the same diagram, for example, that the three considered complex numbers, z, z_1, z_2 are represented in the same complex plane forming a triangle. That is, we construct an agglomerative representation.

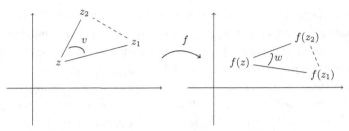

Figure 13 A geometric representation of the condition to be a complex function.

In addition, the representation formed clearly depends on the possibility to form two-dimensional displays.

To sum up, we have observed that mathematical free rides depend on a variety of characterising properties of diagrams. One is the possibility of forming two-dimensional displays, that is, a consequence of the appearance and syntax of diagrams. Second, I noted the multiple readability of diagrams which is made possible because diagrams need not come with a fixed semantics. Thirdly, is the possibility to form agglomerative representations that was mentioned among the uses of a diagram. The last mentioned feature, that of token versus type reference, is mixed in the considered cases. The z shown in Figure 13 refers as a type so as to tell us that $f(z)$ is the value of this particular z whereas the line segments should be taken as tokens.

3.3.3 Observing and Manipulating Iconic Representations

Free rides are obtained by representing certain information and observing the result. This can be considered as a special case of the more general case of constructing and manipulating (or experimenting on) iconic representations. In order to explain what this means, we present a few details about iconic representations as they are used in mathematics. Recall that a representation is a sign that stands for some entity, or object, to somebody, the 'interpretant'. That is, a representation is a triad. When referring to iconic representations, we are considering the relation between the sign and the object it stands for, that is, in which capacity the sign accomplishes standing for the object(s) it represents. According to Peirce, there are three main possibilities, referred to as icons, indices and symbols. Icons represent because they share some kind of likeness with what they represent. A drawn rectangle could be an iconic representation of the shape of my floor. Indices represent because they are either physically connected with what they represent, as in smoke indicating fire, or because of a 'purposeful connection'. The latter occurs when we name, for example, a particular set 'A' allowing us to refer to and reason about this set. Symbols are signs that represent their objects by conventions. Words are symbols as are the signs like '·' and '=' that we use in mathematics.

The characterisation of iconic signs, that they represent by likeness, has been criticised, most notably by Goodman (1976). Goodman argues, among other points, that since a similarity relation is an equivalence relation while representation is not, signs cannot represent because of likeness.[47] This objection does not take into account that an icon is also a sign. The latter presupposes an intention: someone is taking the sign as representing an object with a specific purpose. This entails that a sign (no matter what type) is neither reflexive, symmetric, nor transitive.[48] I refer to Stjernfelt (2007, Section 3) for a detailed discussion.

The icons used in mathematics rarely resemble as images; they typically express characterising properties of objects or relations between them and according to some convention (as noted in the case of Euler diagrams representing relations between sets). But they are still icons in the sense that they convey ideas of what they represent. In fact, this is an important characteristic of an icon:

> For a great distinguishing property of an icon is that by the direct observation of it other truths concerning its object can be discovered than those which suffice to determine its construction. (CP 2.279)[49]

Note also that iconic representations need not take the form of diagrams (as they are usually conceived) – algebraic, or formal, expressions act equally well as icons. To see how, we consider the following simple example about numbers. A characterising property of an odd number is that it always has remainder one when dividing it by two. This fact can be represented iconically by the expression $2k + 1$, for $k \in \mathbb{Z}$. Writing odd numbers in this way makes it possible for us to discover further of their properties. I might be interested in knowing something about the square of an odd number. Representing an odd number as shown, squaring it and manipulating the signs according to stipulated rules, I obtain the following:

$$(2k + 1)^2 = 4k^2 + 4k + 1 = 2(2k^2 + 2k) + 1. \tag{1}$$

---

[47] Goodman's' objection includes the observation that representations are not reflexive; they do not represent themselves. Furthermore, any two objects may be like each other in some way – but clearly this does not entail that they are representations of each other.

[48] The drawn rectangle, considered as a representation of my floor, could be used to design a pattern for a tiling. It is less likely that I would use the floor as a representation of a rectangle (although I could imagine situations where it could make sense).

[49] The reference is to the Collected Papers of Charles Sanders Peirce (Peirce 1965–67), book 2, paragraph 279.

Observing the last expression, I notice that it also has the form of an odd number. Thus, representing a mathematical situation (such as an object or relations between objects) iconically and manipulating, or experimenting with, the signs may lead to a new insight. Sometimes when representing certain facts, a conclusion may even be read off immediately as in the case of free rides.

Peirce emphasises this feature of iconic representations. In 'On the algebra of logic. A contribution to the philosophy of notation' (published in 1885) he describes how observing signs leads to new discoveries in mathematics:[50]

> The truth, however, appears to be that all deductive reasoning, even simple syllogism, involves an element of observation; namely, deduction consists in constructing an icon or diagram the relations of whose parts shall present a complete analogy with those of the parts of the object of reasoning, of experimenting upon this image in the imagination, and of observing the result so as to discover unnoticed and hidden relations among the parts. ... As for algebra, the very idea of the art is that it presents formulae which can be manipulated, and that by observing the effects of such manipulation we find properties not to be otherwise discerned. (CP 3.363)

We end this section by two examples that illustrate different ways that icons lead to new insight. The first considers a case of representing a situation in a richer context where new properties become visible. In this case it is possible to re-interpret these properties in the represented configuration (what I have referred to as the target). In the second case that is not possible, that is, the representation gives rise to new concepts and properties that do not correspond to anything in the represented situation and give rise to completely new domains or theories. Recall that when constructing representations, a correspondence is set up saying which objects, properties, relations, and so on, of the target situation correspond to which (visual) features of the representation.

The first example shows how representing natural numbers in a richer context allows us to determine, or discover if you prefer, Pythagorean triples. In this case, we represent numbers geometrically by points as seen in Figure 14. The convention is that each point represents a unit. The representation further exploits the two-dimensionality of the plane to arrange points in the shape of geometric figures. The intention is first to display a square corresponding to the number c^2; see Figure 14. Considering the geometric representation on the right then reveals that it is possible to cut up the larger square into a square

---

[50] Peirce refers to the notion of 'diagrammatic reasoning' which is his way of characterising the necessary reasoning that is characteristic for mathematics. 'Diagram' is here used in a special technical sense and does not refer to what we would normally take a diagram to be. A Peircean diagram is an iconic representation that displays logical relations. See Stjernfelt (2007) and Carter (2020) for further elaborations.

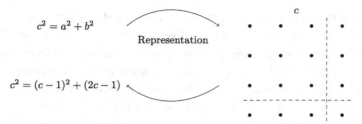

$$c^2 = a^2 + b^2$$

Representation

$$c^2 = (c-1)^2 + (2c-1)$$

Figure 14 A geometric representation of Pythagoras' theorem.

and a gnomon, corresponding to the stippled lines. We therefore see that the square c^2 can be written as the sum of a square that contains $(c-1)^2$ points and the number $2(c-1) + 1$. The last number need not be a square – but we immediately notice that it is an odd number. If we then search for numbers c so that $2(c-1) + 1$ is a square (using the fact that odd squares are squares of odd numbers), we have a systematic way to obtain some of the Pythagorean triples.[51] Other Pythagorean triples can be determined by experimenting with the geometric representation, finding different ways to cut up the square.

The final example returns to Riemann's representation of the complex numbers in a plane. We noticed that triangles appear, see Figure 13, and remarked that it is possible to derive that the defining property of a complex function implies that the two triangles that appear are similar. In this case, however, there is no immediate interpretation of this property in the target situation. That is, there is nothing in the analytic context of considering complex functions that corresponds to triangles or other two-dimensional geometric figures. As noted in Section 1.2.1 and the end of Section 2, Riemann exploited the geometric intuition even further and introduced Riemann surfaces as a way to handle multi-valued complex functions. By doing this, he was able to ask questions that turned out to be very fruitful, for example, how many functions are possible to define on such surfaces depending on their geometric properties – a question that would make no sense in the context of the analytic treatment of complex numbers.

Conclusion

The 'philosophy of mathematical practice' currently encompasses a range of approaches. This Element characterises PMP as a subset of philosophy that

---

[51] To see how it goes I give the following example. We choose the first odd number, 3, and consider its square, 9. Putting 9 equal to the expression of the gnomon, that is $9 = 2(c-1) + 1$ we find that $c - 1 = 4$ and $c = 5$ which give us the triple $(3, 4, 5)$. The clever reader might be able to work out the formula for these triples: $\left(m, \frac{m^2-1}{2}, \frac{m^2+1}{2}\right)$, for odd m.

takes mathematical practice seriously. 'Mathematical practice' can be interpreted in different ways. One perspective may focus on *mathematics* itself, either by addressing questions that are based on internal or external mathematical concerns or by integrating mathematical results or methods when dealing with philosophical inquires. Throughout this Element, I have provided numerous illustrations. For instance, in Section 1, I mentioned the challenge of conceptualising the 'infinite' and how to philosophically articulate certain epistemic virtues such as explanatory proofs. Section 2 addressed various components of a structuralist view of mathematics whereas Section 3 examined properties of effective representations. All of these are internal mathematical considerations. I have only briefly mentioned external questions or concerns, such as whether mathematics explains external facts and whether activities like counting may lead to mathematical theories (both in Section 1). This does not mean that external issues are less important. The extent to which mathematics permeates modern society makes such considerations highly relevant. Examples include: the fact that knowledge of mathematics acts as a gatekeeper to society, gender issues, and the role of mathematics (or, more broadly, science) in policymaking.

Moreover, I have made a distinction between a static and a dynamic conception of mathematics. The latter is prevalent when emphasising *practice* in PMP. In this case, the focus is primarily on the activities of human agents and how they affect our knowledge of mathematics and how agents' cognitive abilities influence what we are able to perceive in visual representations. However, PMP may consider mathematics from both a dynamic and a static perspective. This is observed in Section 2 where we noted that 'structure' can be considered both as a verb and as a noun. As a verb, we may consider different ways to structure a theory or as a tool to unify, organise or discover new mathematics (using the axiomatic method). As a noun, it may refer to the fundamental structures that constitute modern mathematics. In the latter case, I further emphasised that mathematics is also *about* relations between these structures. Section 3 considered a number of dynamic concerns, including the role of visual representations as tools in proofs in contemporary mathematics and how they sometimes lead to new results. However, to account for the validity of the plane geometry of the ancient Greeks, it is useful to examine the theory and associated practice from a static point of view.

Some methodological aspects were addressed in Section 1. I noted that PMP also employs analytic tools, but that this toolbox needs to be extended in order to take into account, for example, how to handle case studies. An important part of the philosopher of practice's toolbox or skill set includes being able to select the relevant parts of mathematics to study, to analyse them and to extract the appropriate general features. In general, I have underscored the value of adopting an historically informed approach.

The field faces some challenges: In addition to formulating a general description and methodology, as highlighted by Van Bendegem (2014), it is important to maintain relations with the mainstream philosophers of mathematics. Another challenge that PMP should be well-equipped to meet is the task of rendering the philosophy of mathematics interesting and relevant to mathematicians.

References

Aberdein, A., Rittberg, C. J., and Tanswell, F. S. [2021]. 'Virtue theory of mathematical practices: an introduction'. Synthese, 199(3–4): pp. 10167–10180.

Antonelli, A. [2001]. 'Introduction'. Topoi, 20: pp. 1–3.

Arana, A. [2008]. 'Logical and semantic purity'. ProtoSociology, 25: pp. 36–48.

Arana, A. [2009]. 'On formally measuring and eliminating extraneous notions in proofs.' Philosophia Mathematica, 17(2): pp. 189–207.

Arana, A. [2022]. 'Idéaux de preuve: explication et pureté'. In Arana, A. and Panza, M. (eds.), Précis de philosophie de la logique et des mathématiques, volume 2, chapter 9. Éditions de la Sorbonne, pp 387–419.

Atiyah, M. [1978]. 'The unity of mathematics'. The Bulletin of the London Mathematical Society, 10(1): pp. 69–76.

Avigad, J. [2021]. 'Reliability of mathematical inference'. Synthese, 198: pp. 7377–7399.

Avigad, J. and Mumma, J. [2009]. 'A formal system for Euclid's *Elements*'. Review of Symbolic Logic, 2: pp. 700–768.

Awodey, S. [2004]. 'An answer to Hellman's question: "Does category theory provide a framework for mathematical structuralism?"' Philosophia Mathematica, 12(1): pp. 54–64.

Barwise, J, and Etchemendy, J. [1996]. 'Visual information and valid reasoning'. In Allwein, G. and Barwise, J. (eds.), Logical Reasoning with Diagrams, Oxford University Press, pp. 3–26.

Beck, M., Marchesi, G., Pixton, D. and Sabalka, L. [2002–18]. A First Course in Complex Analysis, Orthogonal Publishing. Found online at https://matthbeck.github.io/papers/complexorth.pdf

Benacerraf, P. [1965]. 'What numbers could not be'. The Philosophical Review, 74: pp. 47–73.

Benacerraf, P. [1973]. 'Mathematical truth'. The Journal of Philosophy, 70(19): pp. 661–679.

Benci, V., Bottazzi, E., and Di Nasso, M., [2015]. 'Some applications of numerosities in measure theory'. Rendiconti Lincei-Matematica e Applicazioni, 26: pp. 37–47.

Benis-Sinaceur, H. [2018]. 'Scientific Philosophy and Philosophical Science'. In Tahiri, H. (ed.), The Philosophers and Mathematics, Springer International Publishing, pp. 25–66.

Bertin, J. [2011]. Semiology of Graphics: diagrams, networks, maps. Translated by W. J. Berg, Esri Press.

Borel, A. [1998]. 'Twenty-Five Years with Nicolas Bourbaki, (1949–1973)'. Notices of the American Mathematical Society, 45 (3): pp. 373–380.

Bourbaki, N. [1950]. 'The architecture of modern mathematics'. The American Mathematical Monthly, 57: pp. 221–232.

Bourbaki, N. [1960]. Éléments de mathématique – Livre I: Théorie des ensembles. Hermann.

Cantù, P. [2020]. 'Grassmann's concept structuralism'. In Reck, E. and Schiemer, G. (eds.), The Prehistory of Mathematical Structuralism, Oxford University Press, pp. 21–58.

Cantù, P. [2023]. 'What is axiomatics?' Annals of Mathematics and Philosophy, 1: pp. 1–24.

Cartan, H. [1980]. 'Nicholas Bourbaki and contemporary mathematics'. The Mathematical Intelligencer, 2: pp. 175–180.

Carter, J. [2008]. 'Structuralism as a philosophy of mathematical practice'. Synthese, 163(2): pp. 119–131.

Carter, J. [2010]. 'Diagrams and proofs in analysis'. International Studies in the Philosophy of Science, 24: pp. 1–14.

Carter, J. [2014]. 'Mathematics dealing with "hypothetical states of things"'. Philosophia Mathematica, 22(2): pp. 209–230.

Carter, J. [2018]. 'Graph-algebras – faithful representations and mediating objects in mathematics'. Endeavour, 42: pp. 180–188.

Carter, J. [2019]. 'The philosophy of mathematical practice – motivations, themes and prospects'. Philosophia Mathematica, 27: pp. 1–32.

Carter, J. [2020]. 'Logic of relations and diagrammatic reasoning: Structuralist elements in the work of Charles Sanders Peirce'. In Reck, E. and Schiemer, G. (eds.), The Prehistory of Mathematical Structuralism, Oxford University Press, pp. 241–272.

Carter, J. [2021]. '"Free rides" in mathematics'. Synthese, 199(3–4): pp. 10475–10498.

Carter, J. [forthcoming]. 'Variations of mathematical understanding'. Manuscript.

Catton, P. and Montelle, C. [2012]. 'To diagram, to demonstrate: To do, to see, and to judge in Greek geometry'. Philosophia Mathematica, 20(1): pp. 25–57.

Cellucci, C. [2022]. The Making of Mathematics. Heuristic Philosophy of Mathematics, Synthese Library 448.

Corry, L. [2004]. Modern Algebra and the Rise of Mathematical Structures. Second revised edition, Birkhäuser.

Corry, L. [2006]. 'Axiomatics, empiricism, and Anschauung in Hilbert's conception of geometry: Between arithmetic and general relativity'. In Ferreirós, J. and Gray, J. (eds.), The Architecture of Modern Mathematics, pp. 133–156.

De Toffoli, S. [2021]. 'Groundwork for a fallibilist account of mathematics'. The Philosophical Quarterly, 71(4): pp. 823–844.

De Toffoli, S. [2022]. 'What are mathematical diagrams?' Synthese, 200(2). https://doi.org/10.1007/s11229-022-03553-w.

De Toffoli, S. and Giardino, V. [2014]. 'Forms and roles of diagrams in knot theory'. Erkenntnis, 79: pp. 829–842.

Easwaran, K., Hayek, H., Mancosu, P. and Oppy, G. [2023]. 'Infinity', The Stanford Encyclopedia of Philosophy (Winter Edition), Edward N. Zalta and Uri Nodelman (eds.), https://plato.stanford.edu/archives/win2023/entries/infinity/.

Epple, M. [2004]. 'Knot invariants in Vienna and Princeton during the 1920s: Epistemic configurations of mathematical research'. Science in Context, 17: pp. 131–164.

Euler, L. [2000]. Foundations of differential calculus. Translated by R. Blanton, Springer.

Feferman, S. [1999]. 'Does mathematics need new axioms?' The American Mathematical Monthly, 106(2): pp. 99–111.

Ferreirós, J. [2007]. Labyrinth of Thought. A History of Set Theory and Its Role in Modern Mathematics (2nd ed.). Birkhäuser.

Ferreirós, J. [2016]. Mathematical Knowledge and the Interplay of Practices. Princeton University Press.

Ferreirós, J. [2024]. 'What are mathematical practices? The web-of-practices approach'. In Sriraman, B. (ed.), Handbook in the History and Philosophy of Mathematical Practice. Springer, pp. 2793–2819.

Ferreirós, J. and Gray, J. [2006]. The Architecture of Modern Mathematics. Essays in History and Philosophy. Oxford University Press.

Ferreirós, J. and Reck, E. [2020]. 'Dedekind's mathematical structuralism: From Galois theory to numbers, sets, and functions'. In Reck, E. and Schiemer, G. (eds.), The Prehistory of Mathematical Structuralism, Oxford University Press, pp. 59–87.

Friedman, M. [2012]. 'Scientific Philosophy from Helmholtz to Carnap and Quine'. In Creath, R. (ed.), Rudolf Carnap and the Legacy of Logical Empiricism, Springer Netherlands, pp. 1–11.

Giaquinto, M. [2005]. 'Mathematical activity'. In Mancosu, P., Jørgensen, K. and Pedersen, S. A. (eds.), Visualization, Explanation and Reasoning Styles in Mathematics, Synthese Library, vol 327, Springer, pp. 75–87.

Giaquinto, M. [2007]. Visual Thinking in Mathematics. Oxford University Press.

Giaquinto, M. [2020]. 'The epistemology of visual thinking in mathematics,' The Stanford Encyclopedia of Philosophy (Spring 2020 Edition), Edward N. Zalta (ed.), https://plato.stanford.edu/archives/spr2020/entries/epistemology-visual-thinking/.

Giardino, V. [2017]. 'The practical turn in philosophy of mathematics: A portrait of a young discipline'. Phenomenology and Mind, 12: pp. 18–28.

Giardino, V. [2023]. 'The practice of mathematics: Cognitive resources and conceptual content'. Topoi, 42(1): pp. 259–270.

Goodman, N. [1976]. Languages of Art. An Approach to a Theory of Symbols. 2nd ed., second printing. Hackett Publishing.

Hafner, J. and Mancosu, P. [2005]. 'The varieties of mathematical explanation'. In Mancosu, P., Jørgensen, K. F., and Pedersen, S. A. (eds.), Visualization, explanation and reasoning styles in mathematics. Springer, pp. 215–250.

Hafner, J. and Mancosu, P. [2008]. 'Beyond unification'. In Mancosu (ed.), The Philosophy of Mathematical Practice. Oxford University Press, pp. 151–178.

Hahn, H. [1980]. 'The crisis in intuition'. In McGuiness, B. (ed.), Empiricism, Logic and Mathematics. Vienna Circle Collection, vol 13, Springer, pp. 73–102.

Hellman, G. and Shapiro, S. [2018]. Mathematical Structuralism. Cambridge University Press.

Hilbert, D. [1900]. 'Über den Zahlbegriff'. Jahresbericht der Deutschen Mathematiker-Vereinigung, 8: pp. 180–183.

Hilbert, D. [1918]. 'Axiomatic thought'. In Ewald, W. B. [2005]. From Kant to Hilbert: A Source Book in the Foundations of Mathematics. Volume 2. Clarendon Press, pp. 1107–1115.

Hilbert, D. [1950]. The Foundations of Geometry. Translated by E. J. Townsend. The Open Court Publishing Company.

Johansen, M. W. and Pallivicini, J. L. [2022]. 'Entering the valley of formalism: Trends and changes in mathematicians' publication practice – 1885 to 2015'. Synthese, 200: p. 239.

Jones, V. [1998]. 'A credo of sorts'. In Dales, H. G. and Oliveri, G. (eds.), Truth in Mathematics. Clarendon Press, pp. 203–214.

Keränen, J. [2001]. 'The identity problem for realist structuralism'. Philosophia Mathematica, 9(3): pp. 308–330.

Kitcher, P. [1984]. The nature of mathematical knowledge. Oxford University Press.

Knobloch, E. [2000]. 'Analogy and the growth of mathematical knowledge'. In Grosholz, E. and Breger, H. (eds.), The Growth of Mathematical Knowledge. Synthese Library, vol. 289, Springer, pp. 295–314.

Korbmacher, J. and Schiemer, G. [2018]. 'What are structural properties?' Philosophia Mathematica, 26(3): pp. 295–323.

Krömer, R. [2007]. Tool and Object. A History and Philosophy of Category Theory. Birkhäuser.

Lakatos, I. [1976]. Proofs and Refutations. Edited by J. Worrall & E. Zahar. Cambridge University Press.

Landry, E. and Marquis, J.-P. [2005]. 'Categories in context: Historical, foundational, and philosophical'. Philosophia Mathematica, 13(1): pp. 1–43.

Lange, M. [2018]. 'Mathematical explanations that are not proofs'. Erkenntnis, 83: pp. 1285–1302.

Mac Lane, S. [1986]. Mathematics, Form and Function. Springer.

Mancosu, P. [2005]. 'Visualisation in logic and in mathematics'. In Mancosu, P., Jørgensen, K. F. and Pedersen, S. A. (eds.), Visualization, Explanation and Reasoning Styles in Mathematics. Springer, pp. 13–30.

Mancosu, P. (ed.) [2008]. The Philosophy of Mathematical Practice. Oxford University Press.

Mancosu, P. [2008a]. 'Introduction'. In Mancosu (ed.), The Philosophy of Mathematical Practice. Oxford University Press, pp. 1–21.

Mancosu, P. [2008b]. 'Mathematical explanation: Why it matters'. In Mancosu (ed.) 2008, ibid., pp. 134–150.

Mancosu, P. [forthcoming]. The Wilderness of Infinity. Robert Grosseteste, William of Auvergne and Mathematical Infinity in the Thirteenth Century, forthcoming.

Mancosu, P., Poggiolesi, P. and Pincock, C. [2023]. 'Mathematical explanation', The Stanford Encyclopedia of Philosophy (Fall 2023 Edition), Edward N. Zalta and Uri Nodelman (eds.), https://plato.stanford.edu/archives/fall 2023/entries/mathematics-explanation/.

Manders, K. [2008a]. 'Diagram-based geometric practice'. In Mancosu (ed.). The Philosophy of Mathematical Practice. Oxford University Press, pp. 65–79.

Manders, K. [2008b]. 'The Euclidean Diagram (1995)'. In Mancosu (ed.). The Philosophy of Mathematical Practice. Oxford University Press, pp. 80–133.

Mazur, B. [2021]. 'Bridges between geometry and . . . number theory'. Notes from a lecture given at the conference 'Unifying Themes in Geometry' at the Lake Como School of Advanced Studies, September 2021. Found online at https://people.math.harvard.edu/ mazur/papers/2021.10.29.Unity.pdf Last check on March 25, 2024.

McLarty, C. [2006]. 'Emmy Noether's "set theoretic" topology: From Dedekind to the rise of functors'. In Ferreirós, J. and Gray, J. (eds.), The Architecture of Modern Mathematics, Oxford University Press, pp. 187–208.

McLarty, C. [2017]. 'The two mathematical careers of Emmy Noether'. In Women in Mathematics. Springer International Publishing, pp. 231–252.

McLarty, C. [2020]. 'Saunders Mac Lane: From Principia Mathematica through Göttingen to the working theory of structures'. In Reck and Schiemer (eds.), The Prehistory of Mathematical Structuralism. Oxford University Press, pp. 215–257.

Mumford, D. [1991]. 'A foreword for non-mathematicians'. In Parikh, C.A.N.E. (ed.), The Unreal Life of Oscar Zariski. Academic Press, pp. xv–xxvii.

Mumma, J. [2012]. 'Constructive geometrical reasoning and diagrams'. Synthese, 186 (1): pp. 103–119.

Netz, R. [1999]. The Shaping of Deduction in Greek Mathematics: A Study in Cognitive History. Cambridge University Press.

Noether, E. [1921]. 'Idealtheorie in Ringbereichen'. Mathematische Annalen, 83 (1–2): pp. 24–66.

Noether, E. [1927]. 'Abstrakter Aufbau der Idealtheorie in algebraischen Zahl- und Funktionenkörpern'. Mathematische Annalen, 96 (1): pp. 26–61.

Pambuccian, V. [2009]. 'A Reverse analysis of the Sylvester-Gallai theorem'. Notre Dame Journal of Formal Logic, 50(3): pp. 245–260.

Panza, M. [2012]. 'The twofold role of diagrams in Euclid's plane geometry'. Synthese, 186 (1): pp. 55–102.

Panza, M. [2024]. 'Platonism, de re, and (philosophy of) mathematical practice'. In Sriraman (ed.), Handbook of the History and Philosophy of Mathematical Practice. Springer Nature, pp. 2307–2335.

Pasch, M. [1882/1926]. Vorlesungen über neuere Geometrie. Teubner.

Peirce, C. S. [1965–1967]. Collected Papers of Charles Sanders Peirce. Volume I–IV. (Third printing 1965–1967.) Edited by Charles Hartshorne and Paul Weiss, Belknap Press of Harvard University Press.

Preston, A., [2023]. 'Analytic philosophy'. The Internet Encyclopedia of Philosophy. ISSN 2161-0002, https://iep.utm.edu/, accessed Feb. 13, 2024.

Raeburn, I. and Szymanski, W. [2004]. 'Cuntz-Krieger algebras of infinite graphs and matrices'. Transactions of the American Mathematical Society, 356(1): pp. 39–59.

Reck, E. and Schiemer, G. (eds.) [2020]. The Prehistory of Mathematical Structuralism. Oxford University Press.

Reck, E. and Schiemer, G. [2023]. 'Structuralism in the philosophy of mathematics'. The Stanford Encyclopedia of Philosophy (Spring 2023 Edition), Edward N. Zalta and Uri Nodelman (eds.), https://plato.stanford.edu/archives/spr2023/entries/structuralism-mathematics/.

Richardson, A. [1997]. 'Toward a history of scientific philosophy'. Perspectives on Science, 5(3): pp. 418–451.

Riemann, B. [1851]. 'Grundlagen für eine allgemeine Theorie der Functionen einer veränderlichen complexen Grösse'. Reprinted in H. Weber [1892]. Bernhard Riemann's Gesammelte Mathematische Werke und Wissenschaftlicher Nachlass, Teubner.

Russell, B. [1901]. 'Recent work on the principles of mathematics'. International Monthly, 4: pp. 83–101.

Russell, B. [1914/1918]. 'On scientific method in philosophy'. Herbert Spencer lecture delivered at Oxford Nov 18, 1914. published at Clarendon Press. Reprinted in Mysticism and Logic and Other Essays (1918). Longmans, Green and Co, pp. 33–25.

Russell, B. [1919]. Introduction to Mathematical Philosophy. George Allen & Unwin.

Schlimm, D. [2013]. 'Axioms in mathematical practice'. Philosophia Mathematica, 21: pp. 37–92.

Schlimm, D. [forthcoming]. Philosophy of Mathematical Notations. Cambridge University Press.

Shimojima, A. [2001]. 'The graphic—linguistic distinction exploring alternatives'. Artificial Intelligence Review, 15: pp. 5–27.

Shin, S.-J. [2002]. The Iconic Logic of Peirce's Graphs. Masachusetts Institute of Technology Press.

Sieg, W. [2020]. 'The ways of Hilbert's axiomatics: Structural and formal'. In Reck, E. and Schiemer, G. (eds.), The Prehistory of Mathematical Structuralism. Oxford University Press, pp. 142–165.

Simpson, S. [2009]. Subsystems of Second-Order Arithmetic. Cambridge University Press.

Sriraman, B. (ed.) [2024]. Handbook of the History and Philosophy of Mathematical Practice. Springer Nature.

Starikova, I. [2010]. 'Why do mathematicians need different ways of presenting mathematical objects: The case of Cayley graphs'. Topoi, 29: pp. 41–51.

Stein, H. [1988]. 'Logos, logic, and logistiké: Some philosophical remarks on nineteenth-century transformation of mathematics'. In Aspray, W. and Kitcher, P. (eds.), History and Philosophy of Modern Mathematics. University of Minnesota Press, pp. 238–259.

Steiner, M. [1978]. 'Mathematical explanation'. Philosophical Studies, 34(2): pp. 135–151.

Stenning, K. [2000]. 'Distinctions with differences: Comparing criteria for distinguishing diagrammatic from sentential systems'. In Anderson, M. P., Cheng, P. and Haarslev, V. (eds.), Diagrams 2000. Springer, pp. 132–148.

Stjernfelt, F. [2007]. Diagrammatology: An Investigation on the Borderlines of Phenomenology, Ontology, and Semiotics Vol. 336. Springer Netherlands.

Tappenden, J. [2005]. 'Proof style and understanding in mathematics I: Visualization, unification and axiom choice'. In Mancosu, P., Jørgensen, K. F. and Pedersen, S. A. (eds.), Visualization, Explanation and Reasoning Styles in Mathematics. Springer, pp. 147–213.

Tappenden, J. [2006]. 'The Riemannian background to Frege's philosophy'. In Ferreirós and Gray (eds.), The Architecture of Modern Mathematics. Essays in History and Philosophy. Oxford University Press, pp. 97–132.

Van Bendegem, J. P. [2014]. 'The impact of the philosophy of mathematical practice on the philosophy of mathematics'. In Soler, L., Zwart, S., Lynch, M. and Israel-Jost, V. (eds.), Science after the Practice Turn in the Philosophy, History, and Social Studies of Science. Routledge, pp. 215–226.

Van der Waerden, B. [1935]. 'Nachruf auf Emmy Noether'. Mathematische Annalen, 111(1): pp. 469–476.

Waszek, D. and Schlimm, D. [2021]. 'Calculus as method or calculus as rules? Boole and Frege on the aims of a logical calculus'. Synthese, 199(5–6): pp. 11913–11943.

Weber, Z. [2013]. 'Figures, formulae, and functors'. In Moktefi, A. and Shin, S-J. (eds.), Visual Reasoning with Diagrams. Studies in Universal Logic. Springer, pp. 153–170.

Weyl, H. [1995]. 'Topology and abstract algebra as two roads of mathematical comprehension'. Translated by Abe Shenitzer. American Mathematical Monthly, pp. 453–460 and 646–651.

Acknowledgements

I am grateful to Series Editors Penelope Rush and Stewart Shapiro for encouraging me to write this Element. I wish to thank Silvia De Toffoli, José Ferreirós, Paolo Mancosu, Colin McLarty, Marco Panza, and Brad Wray for their comments on parts of, or in some cases, the whole manuscript. Thanks also to the two anonymous referees for their insightful comments and positive evaluations of the manuscript. I presented some of the material from this book at various online meetings such as the 3rd Interepisteme Workshop and the OCIE HPLM Seminar. I thank the audiences for their comments and the organisers for their invitations. A special thanks to my father, Anthony, for proofreading the manuscript and for his continuous support.

Cambridge Elements $\equiv$

The Philosophy of Mathematics

Penelope Rush
University of Tasmania

From the time Penny Rush completed her thesis in the philosophy of mathematics (2005), she has worked continuously on themes around the realism/anti-realism divide and the nature of mathematics. Her edited collection, *The Metaphysics of Logic* (Cambridge University Press, 2014), and forthcoming essay 'Metaphysical Optimism' (*Philosophy Supplement*), highlight a particular interest in the idea of reality itself and curiosity and respect as important philosophical methodologies.

Stewart Shapiro
The Ohio State University

Stewart Shapiro is the O'Donnell Professor of Philosophy at The Ohio State University, a Distinguished Visiting Professor at the University of Connecticut, and Professorial Fellow at the University of Oslo. His major works include *Foundations without Foundationalism* (1991), *Philosophy of Mathematics: Structure and Ontology* (1997), *Vagueness in Context* (2006), and *Varieties of Logic* (2014). He has taught courses in logic, philosophy of mathematics, metaphysics, epistemology, philosophy of religion, Jewish philosophy, social and political philosophy, and medical ethics.

About the Series

This Cambridge Elements series provides an extensive overview of the philosophy of mathematics in its many and varied forms. Distinguished authors will provide an up-to-date summary of the results of current research in their fields and give their own take on what they believe are the most significant debates influencing research, drawing original conclusions.

Cambridge Elements ≡

The Philosophy of Mathematics

Elements in the Series

Mathematics and Explanation
Christopher Pincock

Indispensability
A. C. Paseau and Alan Baker

Lakatos and the Historical Approach to Philosophy of Mathematics
Donald Gillies

Phenomenology and Mathematics
Michael Roubach

Philosophical Uses of Categoricity Arguments
Penelope Maddy and Jouko Väänänen

Number Concepts: An Interdisciplinary Inquiry
Richard Samuels and Eric Snyder

The Euclidean Programme
A. C. Paseau and Wesley Wrigley

Mathematical Rigour and Informal Proof
Fenner Stanley Tanswell

Mathematical Pluralism
Graham Priest

The Mereology of Classes
Gabriel Uzquiano

Iterative Conceptions of Set
Neil Barton

Introducing the Philosophy of Mathematical Practice
Jessica Carter

A full series listing is available at: www.cambridge.org/EPM

Printed in the United States
by Baker & Taylor Publisher Services